Caricatures and political songs might with us furnish a new sort of history; and perhaps would preserve some truths, and describe some particular events, not to be found in more grave authorities.
                                    --Isaac Disraeli.

English history has great garners laden with probabilities, theories, interests and facts, protean enough to satisfy the most wanton historical desires. The common people of that age were not in the habit of meeting for public discussion, of haranguing or of petitioning Parliament. No newspaper pleaded their cause. It was in rude rhyme that their love and hatred, their exultation and their distress, found utterance.
                                    --Lord Macaulay.

THE NURSERY RHYME:
Remnant of Popular Protest

by
Albert Mason Stevens
A.B., M.A., M.D.

Coronado Press   1968

Copyright © 1968
by Barry Stevens

Published by
Coronado Press
Box 3232
Lawrence, Kansas 66044

Reprinted 1974

Manufactured in the USA

To The Decalogue of Balliol

CONTENTS

The Author and his Book 13
I. Goosey, Goosey Gander 17
II. The Man in the Moon 35
III. The Lion and the Unicorn 51
IV. Humpty Dumpty 67
V. Mistress Mary 83
VI. Hark Hark the Dogs Do Bark 99
VII. William and Mary 107
VIII. Jack and Jill 117
References 135

THE AUTHOR AND HIS BOOK

Albert Mason Stevens was a Rhodes Scholar at Balliol College, Oxford, 1905-1908. A small group of young men including the author, Maxwell Beerbohm, Julian Huxley, and Ronald Knox, formed a club in which the members took turns doing a job of "research" on some unlikely topic which they presented to each other with all the solemnity of a very solemn professor. These were satires of learned academic investigation, most of which the young men found insufferably dull and inconsequential. In casting around for a subject, Stevens thought that nothing could be more nonsensical than a research paper on Mother Goose.

There was a degree of genuineness in these researches: the young men went about their nonsense in a somewhat serious way. Stevens went to the British Museum to do his research on Mother Goose. The more deeply he went into it, the more convinced he became that there was more to some of the rhymes, at least, than simple nursery tales. At that time, this was a very novel idea, although others have looked into Mother Goose since then and some of their work has been published. The thesis that many nonsense rhymes are historical remnants of political lampoons and satires which have lost their original meaning through the passage of centuries is now well established.

After the presentation to the club, the author searched through books of English history over a period of fifteen to twenty years, in search of clues. He had partial solutions for some rhymes. For others, he had complete solutions but knew that he had to engage in some legerdemain to achieve this, and that however convincing it might be to a reader, he was not entirely convinced himself. He discarded all of these, and they are not presented in this book.

Other studies offer alternative hypotheses about the original historical meaning of the rhymes which are included here, linking them with different historical events. (The reader may follow up some of these alternatives in Peter Opie's The Oxford Dictionary of Nursery Rhymes or in The Real Personages of Mother Goose by Katherine Thomas.) It is quite possible, of course, that a rhyme originally applied to one event might be modified later to apply to a subsequent event, making two different interpretations equally valid. There is no intention to present these papers by Stevens as the "correct" interpretation, which in any case is not capable of proof. The historical information has been carefully checked for accuracy, and nowhere does speculation masquerade as fact. Many who have read the manuscript have found it to be an engaging way of learning something about English history and the English language. This is very much the spirit in which it is presented.

Barry Stevens

I

GOOSEY GOOSEY GANDER

"Goosey, Goosey Gander, whither dost thou wander?" "Upstairs, downstairs and in my lady's chamber. There I met an old man who would not say his prayers: I took him by the left leg and threw him downstairs."

Apparently this is perfectly meaningless nonsense. For years it has been accepted as just that: merely a jumble of absurdities—grotesque, a little brutal, and entirely ridiculous. We find it among the nursery rhymes that every child knows by heart. Yet there is nothing here that should appeal to children but the swing of the jingle and the figure of the goose.

There are plenty of rhymes in Mother Goose that are frankly childish; they are seemingly play songs, fragments of old ballads, household riddles and what not. Yet along with these there are a certain number that are clearly of a different type; to distinguish them from the rest, we call them nonsense rhymes. They may be nonsense or they may once have had a meaning that has been lost in the lapse of time. No one knows when or why or how these rhymes were first composed.

They were current long before printing was a commonplace in England. They had been handed down by old tradition from one generation to another and were brought across the sea by the colonists to America years before they were ever put into print.

It is hard to understand so wide a currency for these rhymes if they never had a meaning. If they were everywhere known before the age of books and reading, it follows that at some time or other, as each was first composed, the rhyme of apparent nonsense spread from mouth to mouth all over England. Who knows but that the nonsense rhymes we have today are only a few survivals, perhaps the most popular of a thousand such, that were once brought from village to village by the tinkers, the pedlars and the ballad-mongers? These few, with their original meaning quite lost, linger in our nurseries for the amusement of the children. There is reason to believe that such rhymes were at first enjoyed by the men and women of England. And they would be best pleased if the hidden meaning were an attack or reflection on some person in power. England's popular literature is full of the Saxon delight in allegories, riddles and double meanings. The personification of animals or birds to convey a political comment is common enough; Chaucer's Parlement of Foules is a fair instance. There the eagles mean the barons; the water-fowl, the merchants; the worm-fowl, the town folk; and the seed-fowl, the farmers.

But there was another motive which would help to account for the obscurity, the round-about speech, the cryptic phrasing of a popular rhyme which touched on the doings of the great. And that motive was fear. Only in recent times have we achieved what we call freedom of speech.

Suppose that the gossip about the king or the satire on a hated noble or churchman were too foul or too bitter to be spoken openly. It might still be woven into a ballad stanza with enough puns and nicknames and figures of speech to carry the insult perfectly, yet make it all sound like silly, jingling jargon.

It is easy to show that by the end of the sixteenth century this tradition of political satire in disguise was everywhere recognized in England. Perhaps the most vivid example of this can be found in Ben Jonson's Introduction to his play of Bartholomew Fair. That is a comedy of everyday folk and if there is satire, it is general and not personal. Yet Jonson has to explain that he is not attacking anyone in particular and pleads with his hearers:

> "That they neither in themselves conceal, nor suffer by them to be concealed, any state decypherer, or politic pick-lock of the scene, so solemnly ridiculous as to search out who was meant by the ginger-bread woman, who by the hobby-horse man, who by the costard-monger, nay who by their wares. Or that will

pretend to affirm on his own inspired ignorance what Mirror of Magistrates is meant by the justice, what great lady by the pig-woman, what concealed statesman by the seller of mouse-traps and so of the rest."

That appeared in 1614. Three hundred years later a sensitive soul might still shrink from the prospect of bringing down upon himself such cutting phrases as "solemnly ridiculous" and "inspired ignorance." That is the risk to be run in solving the riddle of Goosey Gander.

On the theory that this rhyme is a political lampoon, we may assume that the person ridiculed was thoroughly disliked and widely known. Otherwise, the satire would be pointless and the rhyme could never be generally popular. Again, we have a right to suppose that the name of Goosey Gander had some special and personal significance. Certainly there is no sustained allegory here; the action of the rhyme is that of a man and not of a goose.

There is first the question that seems to ask "how far are you going" or "what are you driving at." In the reply, Goosey Gander boasts of the favor of my lady and gloats over the downfall of an old man. That much is obvious. But there are two possible meanings for the fall of the Goose's enemy, "who would not say his prayers." One is merely that he would not make abject submission: that would be a very general paraphrase of the line. The other possibility is rather more literal, and would imply religious differences as the cause of the old man's ruin.

Since his fall is expressed in the word "downstairs" may there not be the same symbolism in the second line with its "upstairs, downstairs"? If so, it would seem that this person, Goosey Gander, had himself known a period of disgrace after an early rise to power, with a recovery of his old prestige through the favor of "my lady." To speak freely, the phrase "in my lady's chamber" implies something more personal and intimate than mere political partisanship.

Now if we are to go any farther with Goosey Gander, we must try to locate the period and identify the person who is held up to ridicule. Does the rhyme offer any clues in the way of internal evidence? The words "whither" and "dost thou" suggest in their antique form a date considerably removed from the present, but certainly nothing definite.

If we take the literal sense of the wording "would not say his prayers" as pointing to a religious issue, we are not much better off. Politics and religion have been involved time and again in England's history from Thomas à Becket down to Gladstone.

All every discouraging! But before we despair of this riddle we may appeal to external evidence, and that means a winnowing of English literature for hints and references that might apply to this rhyme of Goosey Gander.

The earliest clue dates from 1533. There is a quaint poem, The Image of Ypocrasie, which you will find in Skelton's works, though it was certainly written at least four years after his death. This is a bitter attack on the church of Rome and in the third part the unknown author satirizes the bishops and theologians or doctors of divinity. It is interesting to find that the characters are concealed by nicknames such as Doctour Chekemate and Tom-too-bold, etc. For our immediate purpose the significant lines are:

> Howe Doctoure Pomaunder
> As wise as a gander
> Wotes not wher to wander --

Now there is every reason to believe that in this case a real person was meant, for in the same poem we find unmistakable references to Sir Thomas More and Elizabeth Barton, though, of course, their names are not given. So far as I know, Douctoure Pomaunder (pomander meaning scent-box) and the others have never been identified.

At any rate, we have a man of the church who wrote on theology compared to a gander in a context not unlike our nonsense rhyme. And that, too, in the age of acute religious controversy which has passed into history as the Reformation.

Why should he be called a goose or gander? If we take that name in the general sense of an effeminate, silly man, with the implied qualities of obstinacy, pomposity, and malice, we are no nearer the solution of the puzzle. Is there any special significance in the name of goose as applied in scorn or anger to a man? Let us see!

In the second act of Shakespeare's King Lear, Kent blurts out at his enemy:

> "Goose, if I had you upon Sarum plain,
> I'd drive ye cackling home to Camelot."

Now Camelot was the ancient name of the town of Winchester, and by the time of Shakespeare, there had grown up a rather curious association of the word goose with Winchester. Probably this dates back to the great annual fair in that town with the sale of fat geese there, so that the phrase "as fat as a Winchester goose" may have been current in a perfectly innocent sense. But a ribald significance came to be attached to the term "Winchester goose" at least as early as the beginning of the sixteenth century. This is how it came about.

The London seat of the bishops of Winchester was a stately house in Southwark, beyond the Thames. All the neighboring region was under the jurisdiction of the bishops of Winchester; but much of Southwark, especially the district known as the Bankside, was a wretched slum, occupied by the most degraded characters, notorious for vice and disease. A venereal swelling contracted in this quarter of the town came to be known as a "Winchester goose." There is no question of the meaning in Ben Jonson's lines:

>   -- "The Wincestrian goose,
>   Bred on the Bank, in time of Popery,
> When Venus there maintained her mystery." (1)

Naturally, there could be no viler insult to a man of Winchester than to call him a goose. No doubt Shakespeare meant just that when he wrote the speech of Kent in King Lear. The same affront is found in Troilus and Cressida. Pandarus, in the epilogue, is addressing the audience with cynical ribaldry and tells them:

>   -- "that my fear is this,
> Some galled goose of Winchester would hiss."

It is easy to understand that as an insult the word goose was never more offensive than when applied to the bishop of Winchester himself. In the first part of Shakespeare's Henry VI this is exactly what we find. The third scene of the first act shows Gloucester in a quarrel with the Bishop of Winchester; and what does he call him? "Winchester goose!" (2)

With this in mind, let us turn back to the Doctoure Pomaunder of the poem of 1533 or thereabouts. He is called "as wise as a gander" and we know from the context that he was a prominent churchman and theologian. We can prove no more than that; but it is interesting to find that the Bishop of Winchester at that time was the most famous theologian in England. He was bitterly opposed to the Reformation. He was pompous, malicious, and generally feared and hated. And his name was Stephen Gardiner. The records left by his contemporaries are full of references to this bishop and their tone is generally hostile. John Foxe called him Wily Winchester. (3) James Sawtry classed him with venomous virulent vipers. An unknown commentator wrote of him as Doctor Doubleface and a common cutthroat. John Knox did not hesitate to name him as a bloody beast and Son of Satan. John Rogers called him the bloody butcherly bishop. When Gardiner had charge of gathering provisions for the army under Henry VIII, the people nicknamed him Stephen Stockfish. (4)

It is quite clear that alliteration was the vogue at that period in the gentle art of calling names. Edward Hake ignored this fashion long enough to use the epithet of "Romishe goose." (5)

In short, we know that Gardiner was cordially detested; we know that the Bishop of Winchester was called a goose and we know the reason why. There is no need to claim an inevitable pun between the words Gardiner and Gander. Worse puns have been widely popular. Sir Walter Raleigh, tall and gaunt, was known as Rawbones; and Francis Bacon, who bore the title of

Lord Verulam, and was sorely crippled by the gout, was mocked as Lord Very Lame.

Admitting the epithet of goose and granting the love of alliteration and bad puns, it is easy to see how Goosey Gardiner could become Goosey Gander, expecially in an age when plain speaking might prove to be dangerous.

At this point the voice of the skeptic may be raised in loud objection. Certain conditions must be met if we hope to build up a presumption of probability in this case. For example, it remains to be shown whether or not the career and activities of Bishop Gardiner seem to correspond with the story of the rhyme. More than that, the "old man" and "my lady" must be accounted for; to be generally recognized in a popular satire they should prove to have been at least as well known as the Goose himself.

This is a fair challenge and must be honestly met. What do we know of Stephen Gardiner and his times?

We first hear of him at Cambridge, where he distinguished himself as a student and teacher of Canon Law. Gardiner's ability soon attracted the attention of the greatest power in the English church, Cardinal Wolsey. He was taken over by the cardinal as his secretary, and no better school of statecraft could be imagined for the training of a man who was ambitious, brainy, and not too scrupulous.

Wolsey recommended Gardiner to Henry VIII who put him to work on the intricate problem of how to get rid of Queen Catherine by divorce or otherwise. However, the question was not merely one of canon law and papal prerogative. The divorce of Catherine of Aragon would mortally offend her native country, Spain, and the Pope could not be persuaded to give his consent. Delays, postponements, half-promises were all Gardiner could obtain for his king, who was wild with impatience. Gardiner no doubt realized, as Henry did not, how dangerous it would be to make enemies of both Spain and the Papacy. It may be that he played a double game, representing to the king that he was doing all in his power to further the divorce while he actually connived at the dilatory tactics of Rome.

Two years were spent in hopeless appeals and Henry was beginning to look coldly on Wolsey and Gardiner, who had served him with such poor success. In 1529 the king heard of a learned churchman who proposed to debate the question of the divorce before the universities of Europe. If they decided in favor of Henry VIII, the marriage could be annulled without the Pope's consent. The king was delighted. "Who is this Dr. Cranmer?" he asked; "This man, I trow, has the right sow by the ear!" (6) At once Cranmer was summoned to court and was soon in warmest favor with King Henry.

Imagine the chagrin of Gardiner, who up to that time believed that he and Wolsey held all the cards and could play them as they pleased! Thomas Cranmer was not in the least ambitious: for all his good qualities, he was too pliable and perhaps too timid. Above all, he was an honest man. No wonder Gardiner hated him.

The sudden disgrace of Wolsey changed the whole setting of the drama. Gardiner was too clever to let himself be involved in Wolsey's fall. He was master of the arts of smooth speech and flattery that Henry loved so well and when Wolsey was deprived of his bishoprics, Stephen Gardiner contrived to be appointed to the rich see of Winchester.

If craft and wit and determination could make him Bishop of Winchester at thirty-four, who could deny his claim to higher honors still? In ability and experience there was not his equal in England. Wolsey was dead; Cranmer he did not fear—rather, he scorned him as an honest simpleton.

But Henry VIII knew Gardiner and did not quite trust him. Cranmer, somewhat older, was kindly, sincere, and dependable. To the dismay of Gardiner, it was Thomas Cranmer whom the king made Archbishop of Canterbury.

There were no more delays now. Cranmer broke with the pope, declared the marriage with Catherine to be void and announced the marriage of Henry and Anne Boleyn.

Gardiner was furious. He continued to serve on the council of state but was always looking for a chance to overthrow this upstart. Shakespeare may have taken liberties with the dates of history, but the second and third scenes of the last act of his play Henry VIII give a vivid picture of Gardiner's attempt to depose Cranmer and send him to the Tower as a heretic. Cranmer's only defense is an appeal to the king. Henry turns the tables on the council and his snub of Gardiner is devastating:

> "You were ever good at sudden commendations,
> Bishop of Winchester. But know, I come not
> To hear such flattery now, and in my presence;
> They are too thin and bare to hide offenses.
> To me you cannot reach, you play the spaniel,
> And think with wagging of your tongue to win me,
> But what so'er thou takest me for, I'm sure
> Thou hast a cruel nature and a bloody."

It is probably that the term spaniel has a double meaning here. Gardiner had been suspected of playing into the hands of Spain in his diplomatic missions. Already he was thought to be reconciled to the party of the Princess Mary—called the Spanish interest because her mother had been Catherine of Aragon.

At any rate, Stephen Gardiner, who had risen to be so great an influence in England, was from that time under a cloud. Cranmer took no steps to remove him from the see of Winchester, but for the remainder of King Henry's reign Gardiner could climb no higher.

His enmity toward Cranmer found vent in dialectic. Every theological opinion of Cranmer was answered by Gardiner with more bitterness than simple zeal for the church would warrant. Cranmer was for the Reformation; that forced Gardiner back to the support of the Papacy and an alliance with the faction of the Princess Mary.

In 1547 King Henry VIII died, leaving the crown to his son Edward, a boy of nine. Gardiner's name was conspicuously absent from Henry's will which set up a regency for the boyhood of Edward VI. Somerset, who ruled in the name of the young king, was entirely in sympathy with the reformed religion; under his sway, Gardiner could not hope to prosper. Some of the letters of this Bishop of Winchester have come down to us. In one he writes to the Lord Protector Somerset complaining of the freedom allowed the people in ridiculing the church, the observance of Lent, etc. In reply, the Protector wrote "that Gardiner had seen more than he had of those foolish and objectionable rhymes, but he must not lay them to the Protector's charge." (7) There is a delightful irony in this. It seems to imply that many such rhymes reflected directly on Gardiner himself. What a pity Somerset did not quote them for our amusement!

Was Stephen Gardiner wise enough to foresee an inevitable swing back from this too rapid Reformation? That may be. In any case, he was right in counting on the blunders of a regency to make its ministers unpopular. He knew that the sickly boy king, Edward VI, could not live many years. He was alert enough to keep his eye on the main chance and to make himself indispensable to the next in succession to the crown, the ardent Catholic, Princess Mary.

Meanwhile, his behaviour was most unsatisfactory to the council of state. He was deprived of his bishopric of Winchester, lodged in the Fleet prison and finally in the Tower. Gardiner was downstairs with a vengeance!

The death of Edward in 1553 was Gardiner's opportunity. After the brief and tragic interlude of the Lady Jane Grey, Mary entered London as queen. Her first move was to restore Gardiner to the see of Winchester and by making him Lord Chancellor she put all the power of England in his hands. It was he who crowned Mary at Westminster; it was he who presided at her council of state and issued proclamations in her name.

His first concern was to strengthen Mary's hold upon the throne; private revenge might wait a little longer while he made sure of his power. But Cranmer was marked for ruin. As Archbishop of Canterbury he had held an honored place in the council chamber of the realm. In that chamber there was not room enough now for both Cranmer and Gardiner. Shortly after the accession of Mary, a trap was laid for the Archbishop which he was too straightforward to avoid; without Cranmer's knowledge, mass was openly celebrated in the cathedral at Canterbury. Now by the laws of Edward VI, at that time still on the statute books, mass was not permissible in the Church of England. At once

Cranmer made public a statement that he had not said mass and would not say mass. (8) That was enough for Gardiner. Thomas Cranmer, old and venerable, was arrested, deprived of the see of Canterbury and thrown into the Tower simply because he would not say his prayers.

If we are to place the time for the currency of the rhyme of Goosey Gander, it must be in the first year of the reign of Mary—1553 or the early part of 1554. If Stephen Gardiner is the goose and Thomas Cranmer the old man, then my lady must be Mary, Queen of England. Yet there is that curious phrase "in my lady's chamber" which seems to hint that Gardiner was rather more than a Chancellor and rather less than a churchman of piety.

As it happens, there have been preserved chronicles of the time which show very clearly how far the people were prepared to credit evil of their queen. In Strype's Memorials, we find that "In the first year of Queen Mary, a very foul scandal was blown about of her, that she was with child by her chancellor, Bishop Gardiner." From the papers of a legal inquiry in Norfolk, we learn of "John Allone of Trench in Norfolk, who in the first (year) of the Queen was indicted for saying 'That the Queen was with child by Winchester.' "(9)

Of course it was not true. Mary was subject to the dropsy and was doomed to barrenness; but a popular satire like the rhyme of Goosey Gander would not hesitate to trade on the prejudice of the people.

One phrase remains to be explained and that is "by the left leg." There may be a double meaning here, depending on some happening of the moment, for which we may never find the key. More probably the phrase is taken from the sport of wrestling, the most popular of contests in Tudor times. Even King Henry VIII as a young man boasted of his prowess as a wrestler. It must be remembered that archery and quarter-staff were dying out and boxing had not yet come in. The early form of wrestling was quite different from the modern style of catch-as-catch-can. Men grappled and each tried to throw the other but no hold was permitted below the waist, though tripping was allowed and even the kicking of shins. By the middle of the sixteenth century, to take a man by the leg in wrestling was still considered unfair. Most men are right-handed and in a grapple without regard to rules the right arm would most naturally grasp the left leg of one's opponent. What is implied in this phrase seems to be that the Goose succeeded in throwing his adversary by an underhand trick.

That was quite in the character of Stephen Gardiner, Bishop of Winchester.

II

THE MAN IN THE MOON

The Man in tthe Moon came down too soon
And asked the way to Norwich.
He went by the south and burnt his mouth
With eating cold plum-porridge.

This nonsense verse, with others of the same sort, has come down to us from an unknown origin out of the distant past. On the face of it, the rhyme is a meaningless absurdity. But there is nothing in the world entirely beyond conjecture and it is quite possible that this nonsense may conceal a real purpose after all. To pass an insult under a double meaning has always been thought the very height of humor. Beneath this nonsense of the Man in the Moon there may lurk a satiric epigram, a popular lampoon of a century long gone by.

It is not easy for the modern mind to realize how haphazard was the circulation of ideas in a world that could not read. Tidings of the wars, news of battles, rumors of treachery and disaster, stories of tyranny and the doings of king and court—all these spread slowly by word of mouth from town to town all over

England. Public opinion found scant means of expression. The commoner was not encouraged to air his grievances; though he suffered oppression, he must hold his tongue. Stark dread of the gibbet silenced those who would speak treason if they dared.

Against this power of king and noble and bishop, open rebellion was hopeless; but hatred and bitterness might always find an outlet in mockery and derision, though the ridicule must be veiled and the scorn concealed. To disguise the affront and yet intensify the mockery, nothing could be more effective than nicknames, symbols, and double meanings.

Let us suppose that some event or some great personage were the object of derisive comment and that the satire took the form of the old ballad verse. If the double meanings were amusing enough and the ridicule effective, such a rhyme would become enormously popular and would spread across England in a gale of laughter. With the passing of the event or the personage, the hidden meaning would be forgotten, yet the jingle might survive by force of repetition. In time it might find its way into that curious collection of rhymes that we now call Mother Goose.

If that theory is worth anything, it is worth putting to the test. However, it is not always easy to discover what the people thought or how they felt. Historical documents have little to say of the common folk; the average man of England cracked his jokes and mocked his rulers with no Boswell at his elbow to preserve his sayings. The farther back we go in history, the more difficult it is to trace the reactions of the helpless many toward the powerful few who ruled them.

As a matter of fact we can find actual instances here and there in England's history of political comment in the form of a nonsense rhyme. Francis Bacon in his essay of Prophecies has given us one of these, and the best of it is that he takes care to explain the double meaning.

> "The trivial prophecy which I heard when I was a child, and Queen Elizabeth was in the flower of her years, was
>
>> When hempe is spun
>> England's done.
>
> Whereby it was generally conceived that after the princes had reigned which had the principal letters of that word hempe (which were Henry, Edward, Mary, Philip and Elizabeth), England should come to utter confusion."

This rhyming epigram expressed the apprehension of the people. Elizabeth had no heir; with her the Tudor dynasty would come to an end. In the past, every disputed succession had meant a bloody war in which the common people were ground to powder between the millstones of rival claimants. They feared the worst; but it was not quite safe in Tudor times to voice such disturbing sentiments. Bacon wrote his essay after the death of Elizabeth in the reign of James I. No harm then in making clear the meaning of the rhyme, for no disaster had come upon England after all.

Who could have guessed the hidden significance of those lines? Without Bacon's interpretation of the acrostic it would be classed as nonsense and nothing more.

For the rhyme of the Man in the Moon we have no such interpreter; if there is hidden treasure here, we shall have to dig for it. The first problem is to discover, if we can, the period in which this rhyme was composed. Our first clue is a bit of internal evidence that will help to date it; and that is the phrase plum-porridge, which has been obsolete since about 1700. In the eighteenth century we begin to hear of plum-pudding, and that is what we call it today. Before that time, the same delicacy—a mixture of flour and raisins, plums, currants and spices—was known as plum-porridge. (1) The rest of the wording of the rhyme does not have any suggestion of the archaic. Certainly, if it must date before 1700, it should be at least as late as or later than the Elizabethan age. Tentatively, then, the time of the Stuarts would seem to be a fair guess at the period of the rhyme.

As a matter of fact, there are a great many references to plum-porridge in the seventeenth century. The Puritans of that time shuddered at all church holidays as survivals of popery and were especially bitter against the celebration of Christmas. Mince pies, sometimes called Shrid-pies, and plum-porridge were then as now part of the Christmas tradition. The more rigid of the reformers thought it sinful to eat plum-porridge because of its association with the forbidden feast. (2)

In 1651 appeared Sheppard's Epigrams; the nineteenth, with the title Christmas Day, has the lines--

> No matter for plomb-porridge, or Shrid-pies,
> Or a whole oxe offered in sacrifice
> To Comus, not to Christ.

Hudibras, Butler's famous satire on the bigotry of Commonwealth times, was printed in 1663. The poem describes how the Puritans

> Quarrel with mince-pies and disparage
> Their best and dearest friend plum-porridge.

Another phrase that points to the same century is the Man in the Moon. In 1638 a book was published in London which became immensely popular: this was the Man in the Moon, or a Discourse on a Voyage Thither. Godwin, bishop of Hereford, had written this wild story when a young man and it was only after his death that it got into print. Altogether, it was the first of the imaginative and extravagant romances of a visit to the kingdom of the moon. (3) It had an astonishing vogue; Cyrano de Bergerac borrowed from it freely and there are references to the story even as late as Hudibras, in Restoration times. By the middle of the seventeenth century we find the Man in the Moon used to designate anyone who must be nameless, a mysterious personage, a secret power or a great unknown. (4) Even then, there remains the question whether or not there was at any time a political significance in the phrase.

It is amusing to find that in 1649 Parliament undertook to suppress the printing of royalist news sheets in London. In spite of this attempt at censorship, one or two came out regularly for nearly a year, under the very nose of Cromwell. Of these, the wittiest and most scurrilous in the Stuart interest was called The Man in the Moon.

Whatever the first meaning of the phrase, it is easy to see that the Man in the Moon could be identified with the party of royalty and by implication with the hope of the loyalists, the exiled son of Charles I. He was far away on the continent, with a throng of royalist refugees, but his agents were everywhere in England working in secret for the Restoration. No one knew what he might accomplish; it was rumored that he was to bring both France and Holland in arms to place him on the throne. Perhaps the very fact of his being a power so far removed from the world of England—royal majesty, but in a distant sphere—may have helped give a meaning to this vague title, Man in the Moon.

The Man in the Moon

Very interesting, perhaps; but of course it proves nothing at all. This might be pure coincidence and the Man in the Moon of the nonsense rhyme may have no reference whatever to Charles II. But in groping for the solution of this puzzle there is a temptation to grasp at possibilities and turn them into probabilities if we can.

Certainly it should not be difficult to check over the life of the second Charles before the Restoration and see how far his activities at any time could be fitted into the framework of this rhyme of the Man in the Moon. Did he ever make a descent upon England in a desperate hurry? If so, for what earthly (or lunatic) reason was he so anxious to get to Norwich? Is there any proof that he went by the south and why? Was he disappointed, thwarted, discomfitted? (For, surely, that is the meaning of the last clause of the rhyme.) And finally, what is the significance of cold plum porridge?

It is fortunate that the Commonwealth period of English history has left us ample records of both sides of the civil war. We need not be content with a meagre story from some prejudiced source. Every event, every change in policy, even trivial happenings in London can be followed with remarkable accuracy.

In the spring of 1648 the first phase of the Civil War in England had come to a close. Cromwell had led the forces of Parliament to victory; King Charles was a prisoner on the Isle of Wight and his son the Prince of

Wales had taken refuge in France. Everywhere the loyal Cavaliers were scattered and broken; but there was no peace as yet. In the west, Pembroke Castle still held out for the king and Cromwell's army was sent to stamp out this spark of resistance. News came from the north that the Scots were gathering for an invasion of England to restore a Stuart king. In the east and south the king's friends were laying plans for a rising to threaten the Roundheads of London as soon as the Scotch army should cross the border. Under skillful leadership there might have been great hope for the Stuarts in this combination; but the royalists of Kent were impatient and took the field before the appointed time. This impromptu army was without a leader until a commission signed by the Prince of Wales appointed as general George Goring, Earl of Norwich.

His forces were too weak to accomplish anything near the Parliamentary stronghold, London, and it was courting disaster to hold his ground in Kent. So Norwich swung north into Essex. His plan was to push forward into Suffolk and Norfolk where the cause of the king would be sure to find support. If he could hold the coast of the North Sea in this region, it would be easy for the royalist exiles in Holland to send over munitions of war. As a matter of fact, Norwich had scarcely enough arms and powder to supply such recruits as gathered to the royal standard. The Parliamentary army under Fairfax was at his heels and Norwich was forced to change his plans. He turned aside to the nearest town, Colchester, and prepared to withstand a siege. That was in June 1648. The army of Fairfax closed in on Colchester at once, while three ships of the Parliamentary navy blockaded all access from the sea.

Fairfax, suffering the agonies of gout, had no heart for a long campaign. He called on the royalists to surrender and offered very reasonable terms. Norwich replied with mock concern for the health of his enemy, assuring him that a Goring (that is, a letting of blood) would cure all his diseases. (5) Inveterate punsters, these Englishmen!

Meanwhile, nine ships of the Parliament had gone over to the Royalists and had sailed for Holland. There they were welcomed by the Prince of Wales who came on board, made hasty preparations, and sailed for the coast of England the 17th of July. On the 22nd he was in Yarmouth roads. If he could have gained a footing there and formed a nucleus for a rising of the gentlemen of Norfolk, things might have gone hard for Fairfax, whose forces were all engaged in the bitter siege of Colchester. But the Prince found no welcome; Yarmouth stood sullenly by Parliament, and he did not dare attempt a landing. The next day his fleet turned south, sailed across the mouth of the Thames and lay to under the guns of the castle of Deal, which was still held for the king. There was great uneasiness in London at this threat from the sea: but worse news was yet to come. The warships of Prince Charles began to seize trading vessels on the way to London and hold them as prizes.

By August 1648, the situation was grave for the Roundheads. Hamilton and his royalist Scots were making progress in the north of England, and Cromwell had drawn off his army of the West to meet this invasion. Fairfax was still held before Colchester by the stubborn defense of the earl of Norwich. The navy was further weakened by royalist influence; three more ships sailed to join the Prince of Wales, whose fleet now numbered eleven.

To the Londoners it seemed that Prince Charles and his force had the choice of two shrewd moves. Either he would attack the port of London or sail north to the coast of Essex to break the blockade of Colchester. Norwich was in desperate straits for want of food and ammunition: unless aid came by sea, he could not hold out much longer.

Week after week passed by and the Prince's squadron still lay off the coast of Kent. Meanwhile, the favorable moment passed. In the campaign of Preston, Cromwell met and routed Hamilton's invading army and by the 22nd of August the news of this victory reached the army of Fairfax at Colchester. Norwich lost hope. Starvation stalked the streets of the beleaguered town and still no relief came from over seas. By this time, Prince Charles had no provisions to spare; his own crews had disposed of all he had brought and there

The Man in the Moon

was no chance to revictual in any port of England. On August 26th he decided to sail back to Holland.

His sailors met this order with mutinous refusal; they protested they would not go back without striking a blow. Just at this time the navy of the Parliament was weakened by the absence of eight ships at Portsmouth. Here was a golden opportunity to sail up the Thames, break through the defending fleet, destroy the shipping in the docks, and hold London at the mercy of their cannon.

The will of the sailors prevailed on the wavering mind of the Prince. On August 29th the royalist ships sailed up the estuary of the Thames and sighted the enemy. Next day both fleets cleared for action off the Medway, but just as they came within cannon shot a sudden storm from the northwest drove the ships of the Prince out to sea. All the following day the gale kept up; on the royalist ships there remained not a drop of drinking water. There was no choice but to run before the wind and make for Holland with all speed.

Even without the storm, this attack was a futile gesture. It was too late a day for such a move; Prince Charles had wasted too many precious weeks. Three days before, Norwich had surrendered at Colchester and the army of Fairfax was free for the defense of London.

So stands the record in history; and for our purposes it is amply sufficient. It is easy to place the time when the rhyme of the Man in the Moon must have been composed; most probably in September 1648. We might suppose that it was first current in London, where Roundhead sentiment was most fervent, where the news of the campaign was first made public, where the threat of Prince Charles' attack was most keenly felt. For the whole purpose of the rhyme is to gloat over the failure of the Man in the Moon to join with the earl of Norwich; and the venom on the barb is the phrase too soon!

Deadly irony! Every move of the Prince was too late. When he made his descent on England, Norwich had been for weeks shut up in Colchester. Too late! When he sailed south to Deal he took no action till the defeat of Hamilton in the north left the Roundheads free to push the attack more vigorously. Too late! When at last he sailed up the Thames toward London, Norwich had just been starved into submission. Too late!

After that jeering note comes the final clause of the rhyme of the Man in the Moon that tells how he burnt his mouth with eating cold plum-porridge. The general sense is clear enough: it means the failure and chagrin of the Royalists. Nowadays we should say that they bit off more than they could chew; and to burn one's mouth implies that over-reaching, imprudence, and greediness bring about their own discomfiture.

Plum-porridge, we know, was abjured by the Puritans. Curiously enough the prayer-book, which the Presbyterians denounced as the Catholic mass in

English, was nicknamed porridge by the Roundheads. (6) There may well be some real association here. At any rate, plum-porridge was a diet for Cavaliers and just the dish for the Man in the Moon.

So far, so good. Perhaps we should be content with that explanation as it stands. But it is possible that there is a double meaning here, aside from the paradox of burning the mouth with cold porridge. It would be absurd to pretend that anyone today could discover all the implications in the phrases of a seventeenth century epigram. Yet, in going over this interpretation of the rhyme, we find a nickname, the Man in the Moon; a double meaning in Norwich, between the town and the earl; an irony in the phrase too soon; and a metaphor, burnt his mouth: but unless something has been there's not a pun in the piece.

A seventeenth century squib without a pun? Unthinkable! If there isn't a pun in that rhyme, by all the laws of probability, there should be.

It may be that the play upon words depends on the plum. In the free and easy spelling of the seventeenth century the word plum-porridge appears as plomb-porridge and plumb-porridge. Sheppard's epigram is an instance in point. Now plumb, with or without the final and silent b, is familiar enough in plumber, plumb-line, plummet, etc., with the obvious meaning of lead; there is authority for the noun, a plumb, in the sense of a blob of lead as a missile or bullet. (7) If that was the kind of plum-porridge served to the Man in the Moon, no wonder it burnt his mouth! More than that, the phrase cold lead is proverbial. Cold plumb-porridge, then, would be just the sort of joke the wags of that period enjoyed. And that is not mere conjecture. Here is an example of military humour in 1648: "There are some, whom I have in my eye, who will get more sauce to their game this night than they expected. I only wish it was the master poacher of all, and not a little one. I would never give flight to a leaden pudding with more pleasure." And again: "Instead of plum broth and curds and whey, we shall treat the rebels with some Pontefract dumplings, as hot and leaden as any roundheads need be." (8)

A rather quaint bit of circumstantial evidence makes this seem even more probable. In that same campaign of July and August 1648 great bitterness is reported among the troops of Parliament against the unfair tactics of the Royalists. It was said that the soldiers of the king's army used bullets that had been deliberately bitten out of shape so as to produce ghastly and shattering wounds. They were called "chewed bullets" and one of them is still to be seen in the museum in Colchester castle. (9) This controversy finds an echo, years afterwards, in Hudibras and gives a meaning to the lines:

Their case shot savours strong of poison;
And doubtless have been chewed with teeth. (10)

Can that be why the Man in the Moon was eating cold plum-porridge?

Twelve years later came the Restoration. Charles, now in reality King Charles the Second, had been drifting about the continent, playing the role of a distressed and romantic exile. He had picked up so many of the manners and habits of the French court that to the Englishmen of 1660 he appeared almost a foreigner. Charles II was tall and strongly built; yet his only exercise was sauntering in the Park. He brought in the fashion of wearing great flowing wigs. These foibles are slily hit off in Butler's Hudibras and the satirist was bold enough to use the old epithet of the Man in the Moon:

> Or does the man i' th' moon look big
> And wear a huger periwig
> Shew in his gait, and face, more tricks
> Than our own native lunaticks? (11)

In these lines perhaps may be found one reason why Charles II never rewarded Samuel Butler as he deserved. It was all very well to be witty, but not at the expense of his majesty: the nickname of Man in the Moon had too many unpleasant associations.

III

THE LION AND THE UNICORN

The Lion and the Unicorn were fighting for the crown
The Lion beat the Unicorn all around the town
Some gave them white bread, some gave them brown
Some gave them plum-cake and drummed them
      out of town.

This is one of the nonsense verses that Lewis Carroll worked into the fantasy of Through the Looking Glass; for that reason, if for no other, it is as well known as any of our nursery rhymes.

How old this rhyme may be, or whether it once may have had a meaning that has been long forgotten are questions that few have asked and no one has ever answered. In fact, there is no record that anyone has ever seriously considered these questions at all. Here is a rhyme, part of the oral tradition of England; there is nothing known about its origin; it is repeated by children in the nursery as sheer nonsense. Why should we concern ourselves with anything so trivial and so puerile?

True enough, it is only a nursery rhyme today; but it is a fair surmise that the Lion and the Unicorn may be a relic of an age when popular satire or political comment took the form of a rhyming epigram.

Any reader in the by-paths of English history will find in diaries, letters, and accounts of state trials, frequent references to libelous ballads and vulgar rhymes. Some of these satires in verse have been preserved and were collected by Wright in his Political Poems and Songs. For every one that has chanced to survive in manuscript there may have been a thousand that have left no trace. There is no question that such rhymes were very common; some of them were no more than a reflection of public opinion on the events of the time; many were bitter attacks on the rulers of England.

It is not surprising that so few have come down to us in writing when we realize that the dread statute of treason, with its penalty of a hideous death, could be enforced against any man with such a disloyal rhyme in his possession. (1) Perhaps the danger only added zest to the trade of the political rhymester, for in spite of brutal laws there are references to these satiric jingles century after century in English history. George Wither, writing in the reign of James I, mentions "a Peere that dyed lately" and goes on to say:

> In spite of all his Greatness 'tis well knowne
> That store of Rimes and Libels now are sowne
> In his disgrace. (2)

Yet, so far as we know, not one of all that "store of Rimes" has been saved from oblivion.

There is reason to believe that most of the appeal to the public of these lampoons lay in the double meanings, the allegories, and the puns in which the satire was concealed. It will be worth while to hear again from that same George Wither. In 1613 appeared his rather tedious poem, Abuses Stript and Whipt; in his introduction To the Reader, he writes:

> "Some no doubt will mistake my plainness, in that I have so bluntly spoken what I have observed, without any Poeticall additions or fained Allegories. I am sorry I have not pleased them therein, but should have bin more sory if I had displeased myselfe in doing otherwise, for I know if I had wrapt up my meaning in darke riddles, I should have been more applauded, and lesse understood, which I nothing desire.
>
> "I neither feare nor shame to speake the Truth; and therefore have nakedly thrust it foorth without a covering. For to what end were it, if I (as some do) had appareled my mind in dark Parables, that few or none might have understood me?"

As a matter of fact, Wither's satire is so very impersonal and so carefully interlarded with flattery of King James that we can accept his courage and plain speaking with a smile. At another part of the introduction he remarks: "Our Grand-villaines care not for a secret jerke; and well we may shew an honest wit in covertly nipping them, but either it is in vaine, cause they perceive it not, or else ridiculous, seeing they onely understand it, who will but either malice or flout us for our labours."

In such a period, it is evident that the love of jest and ridicule would conspire with the fear of punishment to put many a political satire in the form of a "darke riddle" or a "fained Allegory." But that is not all. The minds of men are not so very different from one age to the next. Brevity is the soul of wit and if a symbol tells a whole story in a word, it is the more effective for that reason. Today we have the newspaper and almost unlimited freedom of political comment. Yet the average man, when he has read the headlines of the news, turns at once to the cartoon of the day on the editorial page. There, in a picture, he finds expressed some phase of public opinion on a current topic; and the idea of that picture is presented by symbolic figures. The eagle means America; the lion, England; the dragon, China. Put them together in a drawing, in attitudes that are significant, and the cartoon needs no explanation in words.

It is not unreasonable to claim that in past centuries, before the time of the popular press, the political lampoon, circulated by word of mouth in the form of the old ballad verse, held the same attraction for the people as the political cartoon of today. On that basis it is possible to analyze the rhyme of the Lion and the Unicorn as a cartoon in words—a popular comment on an event in history. Of course, this rhyme has been classed as nonsense for a great many years, and it is only fair that the burden of proof should rest heavily on anyone who argues that it ever had a meaning.

Nonsense or not, it is clear that the rhyme refers to the coat of arms of England, with the royal crown above and the rampant lion and unicorn on either side. These are national symbols without question. If any nursery rhyme could fall under suspicion as having a political origin, it should be this one of the Lion and the Unicorn.

In any case, the rhyme could not have been composed before the accession of James I in 1603. Before that time the Tudor dragon faced the lion as the sinister supporter of the royal arms. The shield of Scotland was supported on each side by unicorns; the Stuarts as kings of Scotland brought the Scottish unicorn to replace the dragon of Wales in the heraldry of the United Kingdom. (3)

To be sure these heraldic symbols date back to very ancient times. There is no object in discussing their significance before the seventeenth century except to remark that in medieval bestiaries, which told of real and legendary animals, the lion and the unicorn were represented as enemies to the death. Spenser, in his Faerie Queene, echoes this old idea of deadly antipathy in the lines:

> Like as a Lyon, whose imperiall powre
> A prowd rebellious Unicorn defyes. (4)

It is quite possible that the tradition of rivalry between the lion and the unicorn may have survived to the period that found them for the first time facing each other on the royal arms of England. Under James I there was bitter feeling at the wealth and honors showered on his Scottish favorites. At that time, at least, the unicorn of Scotland seemed to be getting the better of the lion of England.

In our rhyme, the Lion and the Unicorn were fighting each other to get possession of the crown, with the Lion an easy winner. Evidently we must find a time in English history, after 1603, when the crown was a prize to be fought for. There is but one period that meets this condition; the throne was vacant and the crown at stake for the eleven years between the execution of Charles I and the year 1660 when his son, Charles II, was restored as king of England. That period, tactfully called the Interregnum by royalist historians, was the time of Oliver Cromwell and his Commonwealth. He was king in everything but name; many who had fought for the triumph of the Parliament felt that a constitutional government required a king of England, and in December 1651

Whitelock urged Cromwell to accept the crown. (5) Popular sentiment favored this step and the crowds in London hailed him as King Oliver. In 1653 a picture of Cromwell was found posted on the London Exchange with the rhyme:

> Ascend three thrones, great Captain and Divine
> By the will of God, oh Lion, for th'are thine. (6)

When Cromwell took the title of Protector of the Commonwealth both his enemies and his flatterers believed that his next move would be to crown himself king of England. In February 1654, at the time of his triumphant entry into London, a pamphlet was distributed to the people with the apparent object of quieting these rumors. This was The True State of the Case of the Commonwealth, and one sentence sounds like an echo of the rhyme of the Lion and the Unicorn. "The quarrell for hereafter is not between two persons contesting both for a crown." (7)

In the following year Bonde, the Swedish ambassador, wrote to his king, Charles X:

> "There is no longer a question whether they shall have a king but who the king shall be, and so the former difference between the House of Stuart and all the inhabitants of the land is converted into a difference between the houses of Stuart and Cromwell." (8)

In 1656 Edmund Waller wrote his poem, Of A War with Spain; the concluding lines refer to Cromwell:

> His conquering head has no more room for bays,
> Then let it be as the glad nation prays;
> Let the rich ore forthwith be melted down
> And the state fixed by making him a crown.

So, year after year, pressure was brought to bear on the Protector to take the crown that was already in his grasp. But there was a time when the unicorn of Scotland fought desperately to snatch that very crown from the lion of England. Charles Stuart, afterwards Charles II, assumed the title of King of Scotland in 1650 and was soon laying plans for an invasion of England at the head of a Scottish army. He wished to be King of England; he was irked by the poverty, the bickerings, and the presbyterian rigor of his temporary court in Scotland. (9) Reports reached him of the discontent in England at the heavy taxation of Parliament; he was told of thousands who would flock to his standard if he should ever appear on English soil.

In the summer of 1651, Cromwell's forces in Scotland struck north to cut off supplies coming from the highlands to the army of Charles. That move left the border undefended long enough to allow the royalist Scots to march into England along the western counties. At the news of this threat to the Commonwealth, Cromwell turned back with all speed, sending Lambert on ahead while he followed with his army in a parallel course through Yorkshire and the Midlands. Very wisely he chose to avoid a battle until he could put all his forces between London and the Scottish army.

Once more Charles had misunderstood his countrymen. There were many who were hostile to the Parliament and would give an English welcome to an English king, but the old hatred of Scotland was still a real force. Few would join a king who came as the head of an army of invading foreigners. Even in counties where the Commonwealth was most unpopular, the people sprang to arms to fight the horde of barbarous pillaging Scotchmen, their hereditary enemies.

This Scottish invasion became less formidable the deeper Charles marched into England. The army was badly led and worse provided for; there was straggling and disorder and a spirit of discouragement at the failure of the English royalists to come to their support.

When finally Charles brought his footsore army into the town of Worcester, there was no spirit left in his soldiers for any further advance. Cromwell was by this time to the east and south with disciplined troops that outnumbered the forces of Charles by two to one. On September 3, 1651, Cromwell closed in on the town, attacking from three sides at once. There was only feeble resistance; the invading army broke, Charles fled into hiding, and thousands of Scots were taken prisoners in the streets of Worcester. The Lion had beat the Unicorn all around the town!

In all simplicity of heart, Cromwell reported this victory as a "crowning mercy." (10) Is it any wonder that there were many who read a double meaning into that pious phrase? At any rate, this utter defeat of the Scottish army and the flight of Charles justified the hopes of the people that Cromwell would assume the crown of England.

After the battle of Worcester, Scotland was forced to yield to the power of Parliament and commissioners were sent to Edinburgh to provide for the administration of justice and to confirm the authority of the Commonwealth. On the 21st of January, 1652, they posted a proclamation to that effect at the market cross in Edinburgh. This was plain enough for those who could read, but for the rest of the population it was more convincing to remove the symbols of royalty in Scotland. Nicoll's Diary describes how on February 7th the king's arms and the crowned unicorn on the market cross were battered down and the crown hung on the town gallows. (11)

If the rhyme of the Lion and the Unicorn has a meaning in history, that meaning should run through it all. So far, the theory that it celebrates the battle of Worcester seems to account for the first two lines and no more; the conclusion must link up in some way with the first part to form a reasonable whole, or else the whole argument falls to the ground.

The Lion and the Unicorn

The next problem, then, is to discover what significance there may be in the last two lines:

Some gave them white bread, some gave them brown
Some gave them plum-cake and drummed them
    out of town.

As Lewis Carroll used the nursery rhyme in Through the Looking Glass, the word "them" is understood to refer to both the Lion and the Unicorn. The assumption is perfectly natural if the verse is only nonsense. Probably all the world agrees with Lewis Carroll, but there is room for a difference of opinion after all.

Whatever may be meant by the bread and cake, there is a very definite suggestion in the phrase "drummed them out of town." In military tradition, to be drummed out of camp means degradation and dismissal for theft or cowardice; it is a soldier's disgrace, a ritual of contempt and defeat.

That is appropriate enough for the beaten Unicorn, but hardly for the conquering Lion. Yet the rhyme must be taken as it stands. It is a dangerous game to meddle with the wording in any sort of commentary; it is altogether too easy to adopt some convenient reading. That smacks of sharp practice and special pleading. After all, it is not really necessary to change a word of the rhyme. The Unicorn represents Scotland as a nation and so is used in the singular. In the last two lines we find the plural *them*, and that is perfectly defensible if the thought turned to the individuals who made up the army of the Unicorn, the Scottish soldiers.

Of the prisoners taken at the battle of Worcester, four thousand were marched to London at the heels of Cromwell's victorious army. All the town had turned out to give a welcome to the triumphant troops of the Commonwealth. The victory had been so complete and the losses of Cromwell so slight that the Londoners were disposed to be lenient to their enemies now that they were disarmed and helpless. Then too, there were many Presbyterians in London who would naturally sympathize with their co-religionists in defeat and humiliation.

A pamphlet of the time, "Another Victory," describes the entry of the prisoners into London. As the haggard and dispirited Scots marched past, dusty and footsore from their long journey, the London crowds took pity on them. Friendly hands pressed on them offerings of food and money; some even gave them "good white bread"! (12)

Now white bread was something of a delicacy in those days. Most of the people of England in the seventeenth century were content with the brown loaf which was part wheat and part rye. It is not surprising that such kindness should be noticed as rather extraordinary, especially as the Parliament was not so sentimental. What to do with these four thousand Scots was a problem. For the time being they were allowed to camp in Tothill Fields; but winter was coming on and there was no way of caring adequately for a horde of hungry, undisciplined Scottish prisoners. The government even grudged them the most meagre rations. It would never do to send them back to Scotland to swell the ranks of those beyond the Tweed who still held out against the Commonwealth.

After two weeks of debate it was decided to put all the able-bodied prisoners to work on the great task of draining the Fen country in East Anglia. Between October 1st and October 9th, to the great relief of London, the Scottish prisoners were marched out of town, a thousand at a time, to the drum-beat of their military guard. (13)

It seems most probable that in late October 1651 some rhymester of London composed the Lion and the Unicorn. The news of the battle of Worcester and accounts of the triumphant return of the army to London spread all over England. We must assume that this rhyme served as a waggish comment on the great event of the year and was widely popular while its meaning was still perfectly plain.

By way of postscript, something really should be said about the plum-cake. It would be easy enough to slur it over as referring to absurd favoritism toward the Scots by the Presbyterians of London. But it is clear that the same ones who gave them plum-cake were those who drummed them out of town; it would be hard to reconcile extravagant kindness with such contemptuous treatment.

From its position in the rhyme and the emphasis in the swing of the jingle, it seems as if there were some ironic jest in the word "plum-cake." It would be strange to find a popular rhyme of this type without a joke in it somewhere. Here is a free field for guesswork, but at this late day one might easily miss the point in a topical allusion of the seventeenth century.

"Some gave them white bread"; that very definitely means the group of sympathizers with the Scottish prisoners. "Some gave them brown"; that might well refer to the great body of Londoners who felt no bitterness against the Scots but were indifferent to their fate. "Some gave them plum-cake and drummed them out of town"; that ought to stand for a third group that leaned toward severity and harsh measures.

In every war there is a noisy and bloodthirsty faction, often found a long way from the front lines, and the period of the Civil War in England was no exception. After the battle of Worcester a certain number of the officers of the invading army were put to death. The private soldiers were admitted to quarter and treated as prisoners of war, but there was some resentment in London at letting them off so easily. On the 25th of October, twenty were selected for trial by a court-martial and Green, in the Calendar of State Papers for that year, claims that they were shot. Perhaps it sounds too fantastic to propose that plum-cake means the bullets of the firing squad. That would be another instance of the obvious pun on the word plumb, meaning a leaden ball. "Some gave them plumb-cake" would be a rather brutal joke; in other words, they filled them full of lead.

If the jest lies here, the irony is effective and the association with the drumming out of town is perfectly natural. It is not by any means the best joke of its kind, but Englishmen of that day were delighted with what we should consider very dismal puns.

With the death of Oliver Cromwell, the Commonwealth crumbled into ruin, and in 1660 Charles II was brought back to wear the crown of England. Through all his reign, Charles avoided the tiresome and unpleasant, and to his mind there was nothing more disagreeable than to be reminded of the battle of Worcester and the nine years of wandering on the continent that followed that defeat. The year before his death an incident occurred that is worth recounting. Gilbert Burnet was due to preach in London on the fifth of November, 1684, the anniversary of the Gunpowder Plot.

> "I chose for my text these words: 'Save me from the lion's mouth, thou hast heard me from the horns of the unicorns.' (Psalm xxii, 21). I made no reflection in my thoughts on the lion and the unicorn, as being the two supporters of the king's scutcheon (for I had ever hated all points of that sort, as a profanation of the Scriptures); but I showed how well popery might be com-

pared to the lion's mouth, then open to devour us; and I compared our former deliverance from the extremities of danger to the being on the horn of a rhinoceros. And this leading me to the subject of the day, I mentioned that wish of king James the First against any of his posterity, that should endeavor to bring that religion in among us.

"This was immediately carried to the court. But it only raised more anger against me; for nothing could be made of it. They talked most of the choice of the text, as levelled against the king's coat of arms." (14)

As a result of this tactless choice of a text, Burnet was disgraced by a special order of the king and made to leave England in a more or less voluntary exile. It will be noted that no fault was found with his theology or even with his dislike of the church of Rome, for there were plenty of preachers whose attacks on the papacy were not nearly so mild as Burnet's. Evidently Charles was touched in a tender place; there was a sore spot somewhere in the merry monarch, for all the thirty-three years that had passed since the campaign of Worcester. He was an easy-going king but he found it hard to forgive an affront to his vanity. Burnet's crime was nothing more than a reference to the lion and the unicorn.

V

HUMPTY DUMPTY

Humpty Dumpty sat on a wall
Humpty Dumpty had a great fall
All the king's horses and all the king's men
Couldn't put Humpty Dumpty in his place again.

Why trouble to look for a meaning in this nursery rhyme? All the world knows that Humpty Dumpty is an egg. Here is a rhyme with a ready-made explanation and if there were no other ground for the belief, it is enough for most of us that Lewis Carroll shows Humpty Dumpty as an animated egg in his classic Through the Looking Glass. In that story the rhyme is quoted in its old form and Alice remarks that the last line seems too long. Since the time of Lewis Carroll, it is usual to find the wording changed so as to end the rhyme with the line:

Couldn't put Humpty Dumpty together again.

Certainly that makes a better jingle and is much more in keeping with the fate of an egg than is the meaning conveyed by the phrase "in his place."

Taking the rhyme as it came down to us, does it really seem to be a riddle of an egg? The name of Humpty Dumpty is hardly appropriate; an egg is anything but humpty—on the contrary, it is gracefully symmetrical. There seems to be no natural or reasonable association of eggs with walls; more than that, eggs are commonly spoken of as lying, not as sitting. The liability to fall is not peculiar to an egg and when it does fall the difficulty lies in getting it together, not in putting it back in place.

It may seem absurd to argue the point so solemnly. Egg or not, Humpty Dumpty means little to the happiness of nations. Yet there is nothing sacred in the idea that the rhyme is an egg-riddle and no harm is done if that assumption is called in question.

Perhaps it will serve as an effective contrast to quote from Mother Goose a household riddle that really does mean an egg.

> In marble walls as white as milk
> Lined with a skin as soft as silk
> Within a fountain crystal clear
> A golden apple doth appear.
> No doors there are to this stronghold
> Yet thieves break in and steal the gold. (1)

In that rhyme all the imagery and double meaning can be applied to an egg and to nothing else. In comparison, Humpty Dumpty seems inept and unconvincing.

It is quite possible that the identification of Humpty Dumpty with an egg is a nineteenth century affair, made popular by Lewis Carroll and his famous illustrator Tenniel. It is true that there are somewhat similar rhymes in German and in French. (2) But these are obviously borrowed from English nursery books, for each contains the word England, and there is no evidence that they were taken over before the Victorian era. Like many another conventional belief, the tradition that Humpty Dumpty is an egg-riddle has been generally accepted largely because no one has taken the trouble to question it.

In an earlier century we find the term Humpty Dumpty used in a very different sense. In 1699, Richard Bentley wrote his Dissertation on Phalaris which brought on a literary controversy of the first order. All this would be utterly forgotten today if Swift had not been called on to defend his patron Temple (who was entirely in the wrong) with his satire of The Battle of the Books. Bentley in his introduction wrote scornfully of William King as a "Humpty-dumty Author." (3) In another passage we find, "A man must be dosed with Humpty-dumty that could talk so inconsistently." (4) And again, "But we must not expect from the Dr. (William King) that he should know the worth of books, for he is better skilled in the catalogue of ales, his Humty-dumty," etc. (5)

It appears that King was a cheap wit, a tavern scribbler, a man known as a heavy drinker. (6) For in the seventeenth century Humty-dumty was the name given to a potent mixture of ale boiled in brandy. (7) We seem to have lost all trace of the egg; one might as seriously claim the nursery rhyme as a riddle of drunkenness. Eckenstein (2) thinks the idea of an egg may still be detected in this use of the term Humty-dumty from the fact that there are two kinds of fluid in an egg and two kinds of liquor in this popular drink. Believe it or not as you please. To a commonplace mind it seems more likely that the ale and brandy Humty-Dumty earned the nickname simply because of its devastating effect; after a few bumpers a man might expect a great fall with small hope of getting on his feet again.

There is no evidence that in the seventeenth century Humpty Dumpty was thought of as an egg; we may assume that the rhyme was already old and familiar two hundred years ago and if it ever had a meaning that meaning was even then quite forgotten.

Yet the rhyme of Humpty Dumpty may be a riddle after all, but a riddle of a very different sort. Fabyan's Chronicle tells the story of one such nonsense rhyme. Of the year 1485 he writes:

> ". . . Of that affynyte was one named Wyllyam Collyngbourne taken and after he had been holden a season in pryson, he, with another gentylman, named Turbyruyle, were brought unto Guyldehalle, and there areygned; but the

sayd Turbyruyle was reprycd to pryson, and that other was caste for sondry treasons: and for a ryme which was layde to his charge, that he shulde make in derysion of the kynge and his counsayll as folowith.

>The catte, the ratte and Lovell our dogge
>Rulyth all Englande under a hogge.

The whiche was ment that Catisby Ratclyffe and the lorde Lovell, ruled the lande under the kynge, which bare the whyte bore for his conysaunce." (8)

Put into modern spelling, the whole rhyme runs:

>The cat, the rat, and Lovell our dog
>Rule all England under a hog.
>The crook-backed boar the way hath found
>To root our roses from the ground
>Both flower and bud will be confound
>Till king of beasts the swine be crowned.
>And then the dog, the cat, and rat
>Shall in his trough feed and be fat. (9)

Part of the key to this riddle is furnished by Fabyan. The cat was Sir William Catesby; the rat, Sir Richard Ratcliff; bloody jackals for King Richard III. The dog, so called from the greyhound on his shield, was

Viscount Francis Lovell, an adventurer whom Richard made Lord Chamberlain and treasurer of the kingdom. The hog was, of course, Richard himself; this nickname, taken from the white boar that was his crest, is found repeatedly in Shakespeare's tragedy of Richard the Third. The roses refer to the houses of Lancaster and York whose rival claims to the throne had brought about the so-called Wars of the Roses. By the flower and bud were meant the young princes murdered in the Tower by order of their uncle Richard to clear his way to the crown of England.

For that satiric rhyme poor William Collingbourne was tried for high treason and condemned to be hanged, drawn and quartered. Fabyan tells the piteous story that when disembowelled, Collingbourne still lived; finally, when the executioner's hand was thrust into his body to pull out his heart he was heard to say, "O Lorde Ihesu, yet more trowble!" And so died. (8)

This was the penalty for a nonsense rhyme. Apparently such satiric verses were very prevalent. Otherwise, why such revenge? Why make of the author, when once detected, such a warning and example to others?

Collingbourne's mistake was in making his meaning too plain, in spite of the symbols and figures of speech in which the satire is partly concealed. If his death did not put an end to the crop of lampoons, it may well have made for greater care in hiding away the meaning of political rhymes. Riddles that touch on treason, by the very nature of their subject matter, should not be written in a manner easy to solve.

If our rhyme is a political riddle it must celebrate the fall of a man concealed under the nickname of Humpty Dumpty. All the troops of the king, cavalry and foot, were unable to put him back in his place of power. That implies that it was in battle that Humpty Dumpty got his great fall. But if it was fortune of war that turned against him, how are we to take that curious phrase, "sat on a wall"? It occurs in the very first line of the rhyme, where one might expect some double meaning on the events or the persons involved.

There is a rather obvious possibility in the verb *sat on*. We have the old noun onset, meaning an attack, and we still use the passive form of the verb, as when we say "he was set upon by robbers." In early times, set on was commonly used in the sense of attack (10) and in vulgar speech, set on and sate on were sounded very much alike. That pun is strongly suggested by the hints of warfare in the references to the king's horses and the king's men.

Now for the wall. If one is justified in thinking that sat on means attacked, it is only logical to suppose that the wall stands for Humpty Dumpty's enemy. The next problem then is to find a double meaning which will give a personal significance to the word wall.

If we are to depend on literary usage alone, there is little hope of a solution. But it was the common folk of England who relished the political rhymes and satiric ballads. On the theory that Humpty Dumpty is a popular epigram on some event in history we may safely appeal to the vulgar tongue of England.

There is an old Saxon root wal, meaning foreign or Welsh; in fact our word Welsh passed through wals, walishe and walshe before the force of the umlaut gave us the form we use today. The common family names of Wallach, Wallace and Walsh are merely survivals of this early usage. The word Wales, in its first three letters, preserves the syllable wal which must have been used in ancient times with the meaning of Welsh or Welshman. Our word walnut is a living proof of this, for walnut means foreign or Welsh nut. Another compound word that proves this point is the place-name Cornwall, where the last syllable wall has the old meaning of Welsh. "Cornwall was called West Wales and subsequently the Corn (Latin cornu) or horn held by the Walls." (11) This interpretation involves a certain handicap in time. That is, if this meaning of wall is adopted, Humpty Dumpty must date back to a period before the sixteenth century. For by that time the word Welsh is in use everywhere, in popular speech as well as in literary English.

In the terms of these double meanings, the first line of the rhyme would be: Humpty Dumpty attacked a Welshman. But who is Humpty Dumpty? That nickname must describe a man so well known and so thoroughly hated that his fall would be welcomed and his ruin celebrated in just such a popular rhyme as this. His tragedy should occur in a period of English history when the word wall could still mean a Welshman to the ears of the people. Finally, the nickname must be shown to be so apt that in his time, at least, no one could doubt who was meant by Humpty Dumpty.

And really it is quite simple, after all. Dumpty is a variant of the word dumpy, in general use at this day to mean short, dwarfed or squat. Humpty is practically obsolete but is still found in provincial English with the obvious meaning of hunch-backed. (12) Consider the third line of the rhyme with repeated emphasis on the word king: in all England there was no one so well known as the king and none more cordially hated by the people if he proved a tyrant. Can there be found anyone wearing the crown of England before the sixteenth century worthy of the scornful nickname of Humpty Dumpty?

Only one: King Richard III — the crook-backed boar of Collingbourne's rhyme. Short and hunch-backed he was (13); heartless, brutal and a perjured villain; but a man entirely brave, without fear as he was without pity.

At the death of his brother Edward IV, Richard, Duke of Gloucester, came into power as the regent for his young nephew, Edward V. One by one all claimants to the throne were put to death; the roses were rooted from the ground to make him King Richard III in 1483. All who stood in his way or opposed his schemes were given short shrift; Hastings, Gray, Rivers, Vaughan, and Buckingham were only a few of those who earned the enmity of Richard and were hurried to the block.

The execution of Hastings was the occasion for another rhyming epigram. Hastings was denounced by Richard, arrested and executed all in one afternoon. Yet within two hours of his death his offenses were detailed in a public proclamation which was too carefully composed, too long, and too neatly written to have been drawn up in that short time. Even in those days one could not fool all of the people all of the time. Everyone guessed, quite rightly, that the proclamation had been prepared in advance and that Hastings had been beheaded without a trial at the first opportunity. The lampoon that went the rounds was in the form of a punning paradox:

> Here is a gay goodly cast
> Foule cast awai for hast. (14)

One pun is in the clear reference to Hastings by the word haste. Cast has a four-fold significance: device or trick, style of phrase, anticipation (as in our word forecast) and, as a verb, condemned to death. (15) Any or all of these meanings apply in the first line while in the second, cast is repeated in its ordinary sense. The innocent meaning of the rhyme is simply:

> Here is a fine grand work of skill
> Shamefully spoiled by hurrying.

Humpty Dumpty

For all that, there are as many hidden meanings as one is sharp enough to find, yet it all might pass for a nonsense rhyme.

Without compunction, Richard Crookback spilled men's souls like water, so that even in that barbarous age there was universal horror at his crimes. For two years only he reigned, but in that short time Richard made himself hated more bitterly than any king since John.

If Humpty Dumpty stands for Richard III, who then is the Welshman, his enemy, and how was he concerned in Richard's fall?

The answer to that query brings in a rather romantic story. There was once a gallant Welsh gentleman, without title and without fortune, who was bold enough to fall in love with Queen Catherine, widow of King Henry V of England. To the surprise of all, she promptly married this Owen ap Tedyr, (16) as he was called, and to their son Edmund in 1453 was granted the title of Earl of Richmond. Edmund, in turn, had a boy Henry who was carefully kept out of England, learning the arts of war and peace in the court of Brittany. Of course this Henry could put forward only the most shadowy claims to the throne of England, but his absence on the continent saved his head from the axe of Richard's busy executioner. Every other claimant to the crown was done to death and men who had fled from England in dread of Richard's cruelty gathered about young Henry as their only hope.

In 1485 the attempt was made to rid England of the hunch-backed monster who ruled as king. Henry came out of exile, landed in Wales and was joined there by the Welsh chiefs under Ap Thomas and all the forces they could muster. As Henry crossed the border into England he was openly joined by some of the enemies of Richard and was assured of the secret support of many more. At Bosworth in Leicestershire he was set upon by the army of King Richard; in that battle a good proportion of Welsh Henry's men were men of Wales; it was there that Humpty Dumpty had his great fall. After Bosworth, Henry Tudor, Earl of Richmond assumed the crown as Henry VII, King of England, founding a new dynasty—the first of Welsh blood.

Shakespeare has told the story in his tragedy of King Richard the Third. Familiar as it is, there is one episode in the play that calls for comment. That is the passage in the last act where John, Duke of Norfolk, finds on his tent on the morning of the battle a warning of treachery in Richard's camp. What sort of a warning? A doggerel verse; a nonsense rhyme if you care to call it that:

> Jockey of Norfolk be no so bold
> For Dickon thy master is bought and sold.

The meaning is clear enough; but could one ask for a more apt example of the political epigram with its nicknames, its vulgar phrasing, and its ballad jingle?

Humpty Dumpty

There is something rather like a sneer in the last lines of our rhyme:

All the king's horses and all the king's men
Couldn't put Humpty Dumpty in his place again.

The implication is plain that military power, however great, was not enough to save him. Yet Richard commanded a host of twenty-three thousand men, an army greater than had ever been seen in England, while Henry brought a scant five thousand into battle. (18) The odds were enormously in Richard's favor, for besides this superiority in numbers, he wielded all the power of a king in his own realm against a band of adventurers, outlaws, and tribesmen of Wales. On Bosworth Field the king's army was routed and Richard slain; yet the losses of Henry Tudor were numbered at rather less than one hundred men.

The explanation lies in the simple fact that Richard's army would not fight; it was a magnificent military pageant and that was all. The king was so distrusted and detested even by his own following that many of his men were ready to go over to the enemy and the rest were only half-hearted in their allegiance. When Henry's little army was seen advancing, Richard "commaunded with al hast to sett upon them." (19)

Yet, as Grafton quaintly remarks, "the greatest number which (compelled by feare of the king, and not of their mere voluntary mocion) came to the field, gave never a stroke." (20)

Without question, Dickon was bought and sold, for in the crisis of the battle when Richard charged boldly at the banners of Henry, Stanley changed sides, joined with the enemy and led his soldiers to fall on Richard's flank. With this in mind, who could miss the ironic emphasis in "all the king's horses and all the king's men?"

There seems to be one more bit of circumstantial evidence in the curiously pointed reference to the king's horses. Bosworth Field, where Richard had his great fall, has stood out among the battles of history in one extraordinary regard. The king could not escape. It was a commonplace of those times that when the fortunes of war turned against this king or that, he blithely took to the saddle and rode off to gather another army and fight another day, leaving his foot soldiers to hold back the enemy and die in their tracks.

In this battle the king's horsemen were nowhere to be found. Shakespeare knew the tradition of Bosworth; everyone has hear the cry of Richard:

"A horse, a horse, my kingdom for a horse!" (21)

As it happened, Northumberland, who commanded Richard's cavalry, was in secret correspondence with the enemy. All his horsemen were held aloof until the tide of battle turned in Henry's favor; then, leaving Richard to his fate, he swung over to the winning side.

Humpty Dumpty

Drayton, in lumbering verses, describes the predicament of the king:

> He doth but vainly look
> For succours from the great Northumberland this while,
> That from the battle scarce three quarters of a mile
> Stood with his power of horse (22)

When Richard's horse was killed under him, when all hope of escape was gone, he turned at bay like the boar they called him and died fighting to the last.

Time works strange havoc with the memorials of kings. No one remembers the inscription on the tomb of Richard III. But what an irony of fate that Richard, who butchered William Collingbourne for a doggerel verse, should find his only enduring epitaph in the rhyme of Humpty Dumpty.

V

MISTRESS MARY

    Mistress Mary, quite contrary,
    How does your garden grow?
    With silver bells and cockle shells
    And pretty maids all in a row.

Such a simple, idyllic, childish jingle it is; so closely linked up in our thoughts with the play of the nursery that it seems absurd to look for any historical significance in *this* rhyme, at any rate. But it does not need a second reading to make plain the fact that it is nonsense as it stands. Gardens do not grow silver bells, cockle shells or pretty maids; and there is no apparent reason for "contrary" unless to make a rhyme for "Mary." Perhaps that is all it is, just nonsense; and an incurious world has been content with that assumption for Lord knows how many years.

It is still possible that a hidden meaning can be found in this rhyme. A generation that has endured the laborious interpreters of the lines of Robert Browning at his worst may perhaps be indulgent to the amateur antiquary who puzzles over Mistress Mary.

If there is a meaning in this rhyme, it must lie concealed in images or symbolism which in some past century were clearly understood. One that is most easily recognized is the garden. All through the middle ages we find a literary affectation so common as to be tiresome: the allegory of a garden in which are found symbolic figures. The Romance of the Rose and the Book of the Duchess are perhaps the most familiar.

The ballad-mongers used the same hackneyed simile; in 1462, for instance, there was current a poem with the lines:

Wherfore I lykken England to a gardayne
Whiche that hathe been overgrowan many yere
Withe wedys, whiche must be mowen downe playne
And then schul the pleasant swete herbes appere.(1)

In other words, the phrase "How does your garden grow?" would be readily understood as meaning "What is the state of affairs?" or "What are the objects of your interest?"

Suggestive, but rather vague. We have made small progress as yet unless a clue is found to identify the owner of the garden, Mistress Mary.

If, as we suppose, this rhyme was originally a political epigram, reflecting the popular opinion of some past age, it is clear that it must concern some very well known woman whose acts or moods or

Mistress Mary

policies were of real importance. The people might be approving or disapproving, Mary might be loved or hated—but she must be sufficiently prominent to hold the interest of all the people of England who repeated the rhymes of the times.

That makes the problem somewhat easier. There have not been many women of England in the past who could compete with the men of history—the warriors, nobles, bishops, and kings of whom the ballad-makers sang. Of the women in history, the name of Mary was borne by very few, and of those named Mary only one was known as Mistress Mary.

This Mary was the daughter of Catherine of Aragon and Henry VIII, and for seventeen years she was the Princess Mary of England. Then came the ruinous divorce of Catherine, the marriage of Henry with Anne Boleyn, and the birth of the princess Elizabeth. As a result, Mary was declared illegitimate and deprived of the title of princess. (2) In those days unmarried women, without title of nobility, were addressed as mistress, a term of courtesy with nothing of the implications of later times. (3) Public documents mention "the Lady Mary" (4) but the people were forbidden to address her except as a commoner. Even her mother, once queen of England, was required to answer to the name of Madam Catherine. (5)

This public degradation of Mary took place in 1533 and for twenty years the daughter of King Henry lived under a cloud as an acknowledged bastard. The first years were those of the most bitter humiliation, for she was separated from her mother and forced to live banished from the court under the surveillance of her enemy Anne Boleyn. Anne's fall in 1536 and the death of Madam Catherine the following year brought about a change for the better in Mary's fortunes. She was now of age and by making submission to her father she was given an allowance sufficient for an establishment of her own.

She did not appear at court, but gathered about her in her country seat a group of friends and faithful retainers. It was a dull life at best, and the trend of the times was most disheartening to the proud and injured Mary. Henry had broken with the Pope, the religious bodies were dispersed and the riches of the abbeys were absorbed by the crown or distributed among the favorites of the king.

Mary counted as her enemies all the chief figures of this age of the Reformation in England. Her interests were bound up with the Catholic Church and the empire of Spain. Henry VIII was imperious and ruthless; while he lived there was small hope of an effective opposition. Yet the conservative nobility, the Romanists, and the disaffected generally, centered their hopes on Mary whose claim to the succession might some day be made good. To them she seemed destined to be the queen who would restore Holy Church and lift from England the dread curse of the Pope. The chief of this party and the confidant of Mary was the brainy and ambitious Bishop of Winchester—our old friend Stephen Gardiner, whom we met in Chapter I under the nickname of "Goosey Gander."

Still, the intrigues of reaction were forced to bide their time; Mary must not be implicated in treason. So the years dragged on. Mary, in her anomalous position, could not hope for a royal marriage, and her pride forbade her to take a husband of lesser pretensions. She lived sedately, taking into her service girls of titled families who were taught manners, religion, and gentle living. It was perhaps the most exclusive finishing school of the age. Her household was described by a contemporary, Jame Dormer, as "the only harbour for honorable young gentlewomen, given any way to piety and devotion. It was the true school of virtuous demeanor, befitting the education that ought to be in noble damsels, and the greatest lords of the kingdom were suitors to her to receive their daughters in her service." (6) In fact, there were so many of these pretty maids that King Henry's council informed the parents and guardians, very brusquely, that Mary was not allowed to accept more than a prescribed number.

It is curious to learn that the tedium of Mary's exile in the country was lightened by her interest in gardening. There are many entries in her diary about her favorite flowers, rare seeds and roots. She imported foreign plants that might be made to thrive on English soil and there is on record a reward of ten pounds paid to Paul Goodchylde for bringing safely to England from Spain several shrubs and young trees that had been ordered for Mary's garden. (7)

Henry VIII died in 1547, leaving the crown to his son Edward, a boy of nine nears and frail health. By the terms of Henry's will, Mary was admitted to the succession as next in line for the throne if Edward VI should die without heirs. This was all very encouraging to the partisans of Mary, but matters were not really improved at all. The council which governed England in the name of the boy king were all committed by conscience or by interest to the Reformation. Mary was outspoken in her hatred of the heretics and would make no concessions. She continued to have the mass celebrated despite the fact that it was against the law of the realm. She refused to hear the demands of the royal council and forbade the officers of her household to transmit the council's mandate. She was "marvellously offended" and charged them not to declare it or "they should not take her thereafter for their mistress." (8) When brought to face the issue, she declared that she would not change her faith nor would she "dissemble her opinions with contrary doings." (9)

Mary was utterly sincere, courageous, and filled with an undying hatred. She and her mother had been cruelly wronged. She had brooded over her injuries and had taken comfort in a passionate devotion to her religion. It was useless to ask her to be tactful or to

Mistress Mary

act graciously or to conceal her wish to stamp out heresy, restore the abbeys and unite England once more with the Papacy, if only she had the power. All the world knew that the forces of reaction were gathering about Mary as their champion.

And discontent was growing every day. The reformers moved too fast to suit the staid manners of Englishmen. Many of the leaders of the government were unprincipled adventurers who governed badly in the name of the king, robbed the Church to increase their estates, and affronted the old nobility. But the opposition could make little headway. The wily Bishop of Winchester, Mary's adviser, was deprived of his see and lodged in prison. As Edward grew more sickly, the new statesmen contrived to have Mary's name struck out of the succession. She was too obstinate, too bigoted, too reactionary, entirely committed to a return of the old regime of Papal supremacy. Never was a phrase more apt than "quite contrary"!

Victorians who have read the poems of Calverley may recall the lines he wrote about nursery rhymes. He asks:

> And who was gardener to Mistress Mary
> And what — I don't know still — was meant
>   by "quite contrary."

Calverley has his answer to the second query. How about the first: Who was Mary's gardener? Elementary.

It is none other than the leader of Mary's faction, the brains of the opposition, the man who would be chancellor of the kingdom when Mary came to be queen—the Bishop of Winchester, Stephen Gardiner.

The possibilities of such a name were too obvious to be missed in an age when double meanings were the delight of the populace. Here is one rhyme at his expense:

> A Gardner such he was as spoiled so our plants
> That justice with'red, mercy dyde, and we wrung
> by their wants. (10)

William Turner wrote in 1543: "And chief among the bishops who were the secret servants of the Papacy was Gardiner—the noble waterer of the Pope's garden." (11) When this Bishop of Winchester tried to put to death the Princess Elizabeth, another rhyming epigram became popular:

> Good Gardeners doe use for to supplant
> There bad grown weeds, their fruitful hearbes
>   to save
> But Gard'ner, thou, the flowre of Troynovant
> Dids't think to weed and burie in her grave. (12)

Needless to say, His Grace didn't like it at all. His resentment at the liberties taken with his name may be read in his own words. It seems that he had a dispute with a certain Friar Barnes who infuriated Gardiner by punning on his name: "he railed of me by name, alluding to my name Gardiner, what evil herbs I set in the Garden of Scripture, so far beyond the terms of honesty as all men wondered at it, to hear a bishop of the realm as I was so reviled, and by such one openly." (13)

With her affairs under the management of such a gardener, Mistress Mary might well expect a harvest of silver bells and cockle shells. For in this third line of the rhyme the symbolism is quite apparent; under these terms are represented the two great divisions of the Catholic Church. The secular clergy, the hierarchy whose function is to conduct services in cathedrals and churches, are typified by silver bells. Cockle shells stand for the regular clergy, the monastic orders and the wandering friars.

Originally, cockle shells were brought back by pilgrims from the shrine of St. Iago of Compostela in Spain. As all wandering friars were supposed to visit this famous and holy spot, it was customary for a member of the orders to wear in his belt or hat a cockle shell. Ophelia, in Hamlet, sings:

> By his cockle hat and staff
> And his sandal shoon.

These lines are from an old ballad, "The Friar of Orders Grey," which was a universal favorite. (14)

It must be remembered that the various orders each wore a distinctive dress, but cockle shells were worn by friars of every description. To the common people of England, the cockle shell was the badge of the wandering clergy.

Even so, why should they be the special concern of Mistress Mary? Their story is soon told. For many years the monks and friars had been a power in the land. They were vowed to poverty but as corporations they amassed great wealth and vast estates. The bishops had no control over them, for their charters were derived directly from the Pope, and in many cases the cause of true religion suffered by their greed and self-indulgence. When Henry VIII broke with the Pope, he put forth all his strength to crush the religious orders. Their property was seized by the crown, the treasures and jewels confiscated, and the abbey lands parcelled out among the nobles of the court. Monks and friars who refused to acknowledge the king's supremacy were butchered or left to die in prison. Under Edward VI the Reformation held the reins of power, but if Mary ascended the throne it was common knowledge that she intended to rebuild the monasteries and restore the estates of the abbeys. In her correspondence with Gardiner she made this very definitely a part of her policy. (15)

The significance of the silver bells is equally clear. There is a wealth of evidence to be drawn from that age of Reformation against which Mary fought through all her life. Not content with denying the Pope, the Protestants held in abhorrence all that savored of "pagan idolatry" in the service of the Church. The bell tinkled at the mass, consecrated bells rang from cathedral towers, and the radicals of that period demanded that both should be abolished. Finally, in 1547, after a general visitation of the Church, an order of council forbade the ringing of holy bells. At Mary's accession, six years later, there appeared A Warning to Queen Mary. Here are some of the lines of this hostile poem:

> Is this your care, to sett uppe masse
> your subjectes soulles to destroye
> ys this your stodye to bringe to passe
> godes peple to A-noye?
> . . . . . .
> Well yet take hede of hady-wiste
> let godes worde barre the bell. (16)

The same bitter prejudice lasted a full hundred years. In 1621, Burton's Anatomy of Melancholy speaks of the reformers who "will admit of no holy-days or honest recreations, as of hawking, hunting, etc. No churches, no bells, some of them because Papists use them." (17)

During the reign of James I the puritans hoped that his son Henry, Prince of Wales, would live to lead them to another reformation. At that time the popular opinion found expression in this little rhyme: (18)

Henry the Eighth pulled down the abbeys and cells
But Henry the Ninth shall pull down bishops and bells.

Mary, as an ardent Romanist, might be expected to take the church bells under her protection. But why are they qualified as silver bells? Is there any reason to suppose that the people of her time would think of silver bells rather than bells of ordinary metal?

The earliest association dates back to the time of Chaucer. For centuries the devout of England thronged to the shrine of Thomas à Becket at Canterbury. There, as symbols of the pilgrimage, one could buy miniature bells of silver to be hung on the horse's bridle. So well known were the bells of St. Thomas as to give a name to the common flower—the Canterbury bell.

In the fourteenth century, when the papacy removed to Avignon, all Christendom heard of the Pope's bell of solid silver that hung in the cathedral there. Even after the return of the Popes to Rome, it was believed that this holy silver bell would of its own accord ring out to signal the election or death of a Pope.

> Then pealed the note of a silver bell
> And the great city her breath did draw
> Quick, and the gunners paused in awe
> Waiting some portent: for they did know
> The silver bell sends never so
> From that high tower its single tone
> Save when a Pope ascends a throne
> Or haply when Death calls for him. (19)

No doubt the Pope could afford bells of solid silver, but that was more than could be expected of churches or even cathedrals. However, the faithful were wont to contribute silver to be melted into the bell-metal to enhance its tone. How common this practice was in England is revealed by the events of 1552.

While Edward VI was slowly dying, the country was suffering from a financial crisis. Under the Lord Protector Northumberland the coinage had been progressively debased until finally the shilling was three-quarters alloy and only one-quarter silver. Prices rose, foreign exchange was prohibitive, and all precious metal was at a premium. The government was deep in debt but to restore the currency to a proper standard, silver bullion must be had at any cost. It was decided to wring from the church the little that remained of its former wealth. "Bells, rich in silver, still hung silent in remote church towers or were buried in vaults.... All these were valuable and might be secured and the Protestants could be persuaded into applause at the spoiling of the house of Baal.... Some few peals of bells were spared for a time but only under condition of silence." (20) And so for the last six months of Edward's feeble life there never was heard throughout all England the silvery note of a church bell. Then Edward died and after the pitiful episode of Lady Jane Grey, Mary was proclaimed queen of the realm in London on the nineteenth of July, 1553.

The people shouted: God save the Queen! and "above the human cries, the long silent church bells clashed again into life; first began St. Paul's where happy chance had saved them from destruction; then one by one, every peal which had been spared caught up the sound, and through the summer evening and the summer night and all the next day, the metal tongues from tower and steeple gave voice to England's gladness." (21)

Again the church bells pealed when Mary made her first entry into London on the third of August. Her first act was to stop at the Tower to release Gardiner and make him the head of her council. With her was the Princess Elizabeth and behind them rode a hundred and eighty ladies, while "all the crafts of London stood in a row with ther banars and stremers hangyd over ther heads." (22) Is it unreasonable to suppose that many of these ladies were pretty maids who had lived with Mistress Mary in her adversity and were now sharing in her triumph? A tempting supposition, but no one knows.

Queen Mary was given a cordial welcome even by those who had grave misgivings as to her policy. The nation had endured six years of blundering under Edward and rejoiced now at the prospect of a stable government. At the death of Edward VI it seemed that England would have another disputed succession and one more bloody civil war; that threat was now past and gone. For perhaps three weeks Mary held the hearts of her subjects. But by September 1553, the project of her marriage to Philip of Spain became public and a sudden wave of unpopularity swept over the court. Even before the burning of the heretics, Mary was cursed all over England for betraying the nation into the hands of Spain. Gardiner's house in Southwark was attacked and a plot to murder him was discovered. Libels, lampoons and seditious writings multiplied. They were found even in the queen's bedroom, where they had been left by some mysterious agency. (23) The hatred of Spain had wiped out even the religious differences among the people.

Nothing in the rhyme of Mistress Mary suggests this flame of nationalism. It would be a reasonable conjecture that it was composed in August 1553, shortly after the Queen's entrance into London and before it was known that Mary would marry Philip. A paraphrase might be worded: "Mary, once in disgrace, now queen and pledged to reaction, what may we expect of you and your chancellor Gardiner? The mass is to be restored and the Catholic Church in England reconciled to the Pope of Rome. The monasteries will be rebuilt and the religious orders revived. The women who shared Mary's exile are to share the honors of her court."

VI

HARK HARK

> Hark, hark, the dogs do bark
> The beggars are coming to town
> Some in rags and some in tags
> And some in velvet gown.

The analysis of this rhyme calls for no great ingenuity. There is no obvious pun, no nickname, no central personage to be tracked through the by-ways of history. But the paradox in the last line is highly significant. Why, in any age, should beggars wear gowns of velvet? It is quite easy to show that this is a folk-rhyme voicing a satire against an offending class or group of individuals.

There is a strong hint of hostility in the barking of the dogs; and with good reason, for the vagabonds of rural England had an evil reputation. For centuries there was nothing like police protection outside of the larger cities; every man must guard his house against such rogues as wandered along the highroads from village to village. Great stretches of moorland and forest separated town from town. Outlaws from one county would take refuge in the woods and hills of the next, or set out along the highway bound for some spot beyond the reach of the sheriff. Soldiers who had fought in the wars drifted all their lives showing their scars and asking alms in town after town. The half-wit, the lazy, the incorrigible rascal of any parish would be tempted to try the luck of the open road, begging in the name of Christian charity. In any age a beggar will turn thief with small compunction, and everywhere fierce dogs were kept to protect the households of those who were honest and hard-working.

The plague of beggars was bad enough when England prospered. With a failure of crops the yeoman could not pay the rent of his land. The unfortunate, the failure, the dispossessed had no choice but to join the army of the unemployed, which in those days meant the stream of beggars along the roads of England.

Something was done about it, of course, but with slight effect. As far back as 1495, laws were passed to punish all "vagaboundes idell and suspecte persons," but after the stocks and a diet of bread and water, the rogues were turned out of one town to make their way to another. As years went on, punishments were made more severe for the "sturdy beggars" but there remained unsolved the great problem of what to do with those who could not or would not work.

The poor-laws of Elizabeth made the parish responsible for the care of the indigent. That legislation may have helped keep the beggars off the highroad; but an economic trend of the times depleted the ranks of the vagabonds. The great awakening of England in the sixteenth century, the growth of the towns into cities, and the development of commerce, exploration and adventure all contributed to open fields of action for the restless and the discontented. By 1600 law and order, after a fashion, could be found all over England. "The panic terror that in Plantagenet and Tudor days rushed through every room in the lonely farmstead and every house in the hamlet when the growling of the watchdogs proclaimed that 'the beggars were coming to town' had become a memory and a nursery tale." (1)

Accordingly, the date of the rhyme must be earlier than 1600. The reference to velvet gowns puts back the date another half century, for in Elizabethan times travellers, however magnificent, no longer wore such cumbrous robes of state. The gown was once the badge of the great and powerful. It has survived to our day, but only in the academic robes of the universities. Anyone who has watched the procession of a college faculty on commencement day, in doctors' gowns with velvet hoods, may appreciate the absurdity of such a dress beside the rags and tags of wayside beggars.

The rhyme must be later than 1250 because the word 'beggar' was unknown before the thirteenth century. The derivation of the word is rather unusual; it seems to come from the name Beghard given to members of a lay order that imitated the manner of living of the mendicant friars. The Franciscans, Dominicans and

Carmelites, all vowed to poverty, reached England before 1300. They begged from door to door, trusting to the pious souls in the villages through which they passed; for few would grudge a meal or a penny in exchange for the blessing and absolution of such holy men.

Too soon the garb of a monk or friar became a facile disguise for the lazy and worthless wanderer; and those without the robe might pretend that they too were engaged in holy work as lay followers of the saintly Lambert le Begue.

Even among the real friars there was too often a sordid element. The religious life offered to some men an escape from hard work, a release from service in war, a chance to live without care. As years went on, their poverty became a jest to the ungodly. Men dying in terror of purgatory would leave large sums to ensure that masses were said for the good of their souls. There was always a friar at hand to shrive them and always an abbey nearby that needed an endowment. The estates of the mendicant orders grew rich, the friars grew careless and self-indulgent. Penances were forgotten and the jolly brothers lived at their ease, drinking and feasting in their stately abbeys.

The priors and abbots were harsh landlords to the peasants who tilled the fields of their estates. They were hand in glove with the nobles who oppressed the countryside. When they went abroad, they dressed like lords; and as early as 1342 the council of London reproached the religious for wearing clothing "fit rather for knights than for clerks." (2)

This wealth of the monks seemed utterly at variance with the professions of their vows. Their pride and arrogance were equally unholy. Their power was dreaded, their wealth was envied, and their insolence was resented all over England.

The early reformers under Wycliffe made the most of this dislike of the monastic orders. In 1401 appeared "Jacke Upland," a Lollard poem against the friars. Here are some of the lines:

> Freer, what charitie is this
> to overcharge the people by mightie begging,
> under colour of preaching,
> or praying, or masses singing?
>   *   *   * *   *
> Freer, what charity is this
> to the people to lie,
> and say that ye follow Christ in povertie
> more than other men done?
> And yet in curious and costly housing
> and fine and precious clothing,
> and delicious and liking feeding,
> and in treasure and jewels,
> and rich ornaments,
> freers passen lords
> and other rich worldly men. (3)

If these are the beggars in velvet gowns, there is no difficulty in getting the original meaning of the nursery rhyme. It is a fling at the wealth of the church, but it is a general satire which might have been true enough and popular enough at any time over a period of about two hundred years. With no reference to particular persons or events, it may not be easy to date the rhyme.

At any rate, we should not expect such a rhyme after 1540. Henry VIII was nothing if not thorough. His determination to despoil the church of its wealth was supported by the general discontent and the hatred of the monasteries. The dissolution of the religious orders began in 1536 and in four years the devastation was complete. The power of the church was humbled in the dust a scant twenty years after it had reached its greatest height of wealth and pride. Under Wolsey, the nation was governed by an ecclesiastic who saw to it that the church need fear no antagonist. He himself displayed every form of magnificence in his palace, his jewels and his robes of state. In 1520 it was written of Wolsey that "by example of his pride, priestes and all spirituall persones waxed so proude, that thei ware velvet and silke, bothe in gounes, iachettes, doublettes and shoes." (4)

In November 1529 London was flooded with copies of a little book, A Supplicacyon for the Beggers. This was a virulent attack on the corruption of the church and according to Bishop Burnet, "it took mightily."

The author, Simon Fish, complains to the king that the sick, the poor, and the needy beggars are starving because of the "counterfeit holy, and ydell beggers... Bishopes, Abbottes, Priours, Deacons, Archedeacons, Suffraganes, Prestes, Monkes, Chanons, Freres, Pardoners and Somners. And who is abill to nombre this idell ravinous sort whiche (setting all labour a side) have begged so importunatly that they have gotten ynto theyre hondes more than the therd part of all your realm."

Honest Hugh Latimer, preaching at Paul's Cross in 1536, contended that "Bishops, abbots, with such others, should not have so many servants, nor so many dishes; but to go to their first foundation, and keep hospitality to feed the needy people—not jolly fellows, with golden chains and velvet gowns." (5)

It would be natural to think that our rhyme, "Hark, hark, the dogs do bark," was current at the time when the agitation against the wealth of the clergy was at its height and the satiric epithet of "beggar" was most commonly accepted. However, there is a reference in history which suggests that our rhyme was known before the appearance of the Supplicacyon for the Beggers. Richard Fox, bishop of Winchester, who died in 1528, wrote in his old age to Wolsey that he had lost hope of correcting the corruption in the church. He says further: "The reformation of the clergy and all sacred matters will please the people who have been long barking at them." (6)

It would seem that the bishop had heard the same rhyme in the mouths of the people that now we hear only from the lips of little children.

VII

WILLIAM AND MARY

William and Mary and George and Anne
Four such children had never a man
They put their father to flight and shame
And called their brother a shocking bad name. (1)

It would be hard to imagine that this Mother Goose rhyme was composed for the edification of children. It is even surprising that such an instance of unfilial behavior should be admitted to the nursery at all. As it stands, one word suggests that this version is rather recent; 'shocking' is an adjective with a connotation and usage typically Victorian. Yet the rhyme has been generally recognized as referring to the family of James II, King of England. Halliwell-Philips first mentioned the point in 1842 (1) and Wheeler made a similar note in 1869. (2)

Why should a pasquinade on royalty of the seventeenth century contain a nineteenth century idiom? The explanation is that the original was too coarse for the taste of a later generation—even popular rhymes came under the influence of Bowdler—and a polite revision was the result. For this rhyme we need not depend on guesswork as the older form of the rhyme has come down to us with the frank phrasing of two hundred years ago:

> William and Mary, George and Anne
> Four such children never had man:
> They turned their father out of door,
> And called their brother the son of a whore. (3)

Unfortunately, there are no contemporary records that quote the rhyme with a key to its political meaning. Careful scholars ask for documentary evidence, but such proof as that is not available. Yet there is no reasonable doubt that the rhyme is a popular epigram at the expense of the last of the Stuarts. Halliwell's note was no more than a simple inference, but he was entirely justified for the names are given without concealment and the story is too plain to admit of any other interpretation.

King Charles II had a younger brother James, Duke of York, who married Anne Hyde, the daughter of the Earl of Clarendon. Mary and Anne were the only surviving children of this marriage. The older sister, Mary, was married to William of Orange and there is a nursery rhyme to prove it.

> What is the rhyme for porringer?
> The King he had a daughter fair
> And gave the Prince of Orange her. (4)

William and Mary

In this case, as well, we can trace the source of the rhyme: it is a slightly garbled fragment of a Jacobite ballad which has chanced to survive intact. (5)

Anne, who lived to be queen after William and Mary, had for a loving husband the greatest dunce and sluggard of the age. This was Prince George of Denmark, the royal simpleton (6), well described in the remark of Charles II: "I have tried him drunk, and I have tried him sober, and there's nothing in him." (7)

When Charles II died in 1685, his brother assumed the crown as King James II. His accession was greeted in such a vein of extravagant loyalty and grovelling adulation (8) that it is no wonder he believed in the divine right to rule as he pleased. But England was unhappy and unsound. Charles II had sold his country to the king of France, ruined the public credit, and squandered the national revenues. To James he left a heavy legacy of misrule and discontent; the court was unspeakably corrupt, but there were yet Englishmen who resented the loss of their liberties.

A wiser king might have won back the hearts of his subjects but James II was dull, vain, obstinate, and cruel. As a professed Romanist, he was bound to run counter to the popular hatred of Popery and the first months of his brief reign were enough to justify the worst fears of the people. Monmouth's rebellion was stamped out by the butcheries of Kirke's Lambs and the hideous cruelty of Jeffreys in his Bloody Assizes. No mercy was to be looked for from this king, no redress for wrongs, no certainty of anything but remorseless tyranny in church and state.

There was one ray of hope: James could not live forever and his daughter Mary, an ardent Protestant, would succeed to the crown. For everyone assumed that the king would never have a son. It was common knowledge that James was infected with syphilis soon after the birth of the younger daughter, Anne. All the later children by his first marriage were so heavily tainted as to die in a short time and the same disease was the cause of their mother's death. (9) Then James married Mary Beatrice D'Este of Modena and she fared no better. She appears in Marvell's satire as

> the princess with her golden locks
> Hastening to be envenomed with the pox
> And in her youthful veins receive a wound
> Which sent N(an) H(yde) before her under ground. (10)

Burnet wrote of this queen in 1687: "Those about her seemed well assured that she, who had buried all her children soon after they were born, and had now for several years ceased bearing, would have no more children. Her own priests apprehended it, and seemed to wish for her death. She had great and frequent distempers, that returned often, which put all people out of their hopes or fears of her having any children."(11)

With almost incredible patience the people of England endured for two years the caprice and malice of this typically Stuart king. But there was worse to come. In the autumn of 1687 it was announced to the kingdom that the queen was pregnant and an heir was confidently expected. In the hearts of honest Englishmen there was consternation and more than a little doubt and suspicion; yet the sycophants of the court were never more profuse in their flattery.

About this time there was current a popular rhyme that might rank with any nonsense verse in Mother Goose:

> Two Toms, and a Nat, in council sat
> To rig out a thanksgiving.
> And made a pray'r, for a thing in the air
> That's neither dead nor living. (12)

Thomas Spratt, bishop of Rochester, never lost a chance to play the courtier. With Thomas White, bishop of Peterborough, and Nathaniel Crew, bishop of Durham, he conspired to win the favor of the king by composing a service of thanksgiving to Almighty God. The queen was with child: let all loyal churchmen give thanks for this glorious heir to the virtues of the noblest Stuart of them all. Or words to that effect.

In this lampoon the people derided the servile prelates who won preferment by upholding the sacred majesty of the king's prerogative. But not all of the ridicule falls on the two Toms and Nat. The lines:

> And made a pray'r, for a thing in the air
> That's neither dead nor living

intimate very broadly that the pregnancy was all imposture; it was nothing but a shameless fraud, a trick to cheat the nation of a Protestant succession. Probably the last line carries a slur on such High Church divines as were urging for the liturgy the adoption of prayers for the dead.

The queen was confined on the 10th of June 1688 under circumstances of evasion and concealment that were enough in themselves to excite suspicion. It was announced that she was delivered of a beautiful baby boy who was named James Francis Edward, Prince of Wales.

This was the last straw. Englishmen could not or would not believe the child to be anything but a changeling; they had no faith in the king and thought, with Burnet: "so healthy a child as the pretended prince of Wales could neither be his nor be born of any wife with whom he had lived long." (9) It was said that the queen had not been pregnant at all, or had miscarried, or had given birth to a diseased and dying infant. In any case, it was believed that a base-born babe had been foisted on the nation to maintain a papist dynasty. (13) It was commonly reported that this little impostor had been smuggled into the queen's apartment in a warming pan.

William and Mary

Popular feeling ran so high that the king was advised to call before an extraordinary council all witnesses of the birth of the prince and to publish their declarations for the satisfaction of the world. The hearings took place on the 22nd of October, and never was an affair more wretchedly bungled. If there had been a conspiracy, the witnesses should have built up a more convincing story, but as DeFoe remarked, the published Declarations served as "the greatest weakening and blow to the king that anybody could have struck." There were "so many plain deficiencies of what proof might have been made; so many fulsome follies, surfeiting blunders, such broken evidences, circumlocutions, and very weak low steps, that it is out of any wise man's doubt, that the deposition left the cause in a dirtier condition than they found it." (14)

Meanwhile affairs were going from bad to worse. There were reasons enough for getting rid of King James but this farce of a false heir turned the scale against him. The wisest heads of England risked the Tower and the axe, in combining to invite a foreigner to invade their country and depose their king.

William of Orange and his wife Mary, the rightful heir, were assured of the support of the army, the church, and the common people; George and Anne were in the conspiracy and agreed to abandon the court as soon as possible. In November 1688, William landed in England and brought about the glorious and all but bloodless Revolution.

In this critical time James II, who was already called a cheat, was proved to be a coward. When he found that his army would not fight, he left in a panic for London, where he learned that his daughter Anne had followed Prince George in deserting to William of Orange. "God help me!" he whimpered, "my own children have forsaken me." (15)

William was too wise to dignify King James by making him a martyr; he was allowed or, one might better say, he was encouraged to escape. But there is no question that the king was turned out of his palace in a very ignominious fashion. At the time of his departure for France, James II left behind a written statement in which he complains of the rudeness of the Prince of Orange in "the sending of his own guards at eleven at night to take possession of the posts at White Hall, without advertising me in the least manner of it; the sending to me at one of clock after midnight, when I was in bed, a kind of an order by three lords, to be gone out of mine own palace before twelve that morning." (16) Higgons reports that the very moment the king left Whitehall, his daughter entered it. (17) This may not be literally true but James was so bluntly dispossessed that there was more than a figure of speech in the line:

They turned their father out of door.

There is nothing that points to a definite date for the composition of this rhyme. It could not be earlier than

December 1688 when William entered Whitehall. It may have come into being at any time since then in connection with the Jacobite agitations for the return of the Stuarts.

Most probably the rhyme was current shortly after the Revolution, while the events of that year were still fresh in the minds of the people. There is reason to think that it appeared before the accession of Queen Anne in 1702. For Anne was strongly influenced by the Tories and showed more than once an affection for her supposed brother in exile, the Stuart prince of Wales. (18) It is true that she called him the Pretender in her proclamations, but she was known to favor his claims over those of the House of Hanover. After 1702 it would be rather unlikely that Anne should figure in a popular rhyme as calling her brother that shocking bad name.

But the High Church Tories were never satisfied. They had hoped that Anne would yield to them in everything and resented her course of moderation toward the Dissenters. She was attacked in virulent lampoons and accused of betraying the cause of religion. One of the milder of these rhymes was very popular.

> When she was the church's daughter
> She acted as her mother taught her;
> But now she's mother of the church
> She's left her daughter in the lurch. (19)

Factional feeling ran high in the last years of the seventeenth century. Every man was either a Tory or a Whig but there were all degrees of political sentiment between the radical Whig and the Jacobite Tory. It was a time of plain speaking, for the old tyranny had passed and public opinion was finding a voice in the pamphlets and news-sheets of London.

That is one reason why it is not hard to see the meaning of the rhyme of William and Mary, and George and Anne. In an earlier period the public satirist would not have dared identify his characters; it is a quaint proof of the dawn of free speech that we can read the real names in such a rhyme as this.

It is a fair guess that the author was a moderate Tory who accepted the Revolution but had no illusions about the sovereigns who ousted James II. At least he does not show the hostility to the usurpers that we find in the ballads and lampoons of the Jacobite party, who sang:

There's Merrie the daughter, and Willie the cheater,
There's Georgie the drinker, and Annie the eater. (20)

Apparently there was small charity in England for the squabbles and failings of the royal family.

VIII

JACK AND JILL

>Jack and Jill went up the hill
>To fetch a pail of water
>Jack fell down and broke his crown
>And Jill came tumbling after

It may be worthwhile, before considering the possible origin of this rhyme, to take it simply at face value. Jack and his companion set out to get water on a hill; what they actually get is a fall, and one so severe that their famous hill must have had a slope that was perilously steep. This brings out the essential nonsense of the rhyme, for no one need climb a crag in search of water. If there is a source of water on such a hill, a stream will find its way down and the villagers can fill their pails at the foot of the slope. Especially in England it is ridiculous to go up hill for water, since England is a rolling country of hill and dale, with no scarcity of springs or streams; and everywhere the water is in the valleys. It was once remarked that the only hill-top water in England was found in the ancient dew-ponds of the South Downs and it was even suggested that these must have been the scene of Jack and Jill.

But the slopes of the Downs are too gentle by far for any such tumble as the rhyme describes. There is really no alternative but to conclude that Jack and Jill are represented as doing an obviously foolish thing with disastrous consequences.

If it is admitted that this is a nonsense rhyme of a sort, one is tempted to suspect that there may be more in the lines than meets the eye. Yet Jack and Jill might not fall under suspicion of having a meaning in history if it were not from the phrase "broke his crown." That is so glaring a double meaning, so bold a pun, that it could hardly be overlooked. A man was said to break his crown if he bumped his head; so might a king if he lost his kingdom. Even if there seems as yet to be no clue to the identity of Jack, we have an unmistakable hint that the nursery rhyme of today may have had its origin as a mocking tale of the fall of a foolish king.

Perhaps there are other words and phrases that may be interpreted as having a figurative meaning. The hill has a significance in allegory which is quite obvious. To climb or to go up a hill simply means to make an effort against difficulties, to attack or to bend one's energies to some ambitious enterprise. To fall down, of course, is to fail ignominiously, while to go down the hill would mean giving up the attempt or retreating. That other old nursery rhyme

> The King of France with twice ten thousand men
> Marched up a hill and then marched down again

is probably nothing more than a sneer at the threats of invasion by a French army which never came to anything after all. There are plenty of instances of this allegorical meaning. In Pilgrim's Progress, Christian is shown toiling up Hill Difficulty. The unhappy English Queen of Bohemia in 1654 wrote of her hopeless task: "as for my journey up hill, I cannot tell what to say." (1) In Percy's Reliques an old ballad sounds the note of ambition in the lines:

> Shall I haunt the thronged vallies
> Whilst ther's noble hils to climbe? (2)

Another of 1588 describes contentment with the same imagery:

> I wish but what I have at will,
> I wander not to seek for more,
> I like the plaine, I clime no hill. (3)

Even today we have phrases that express the same idea. A hard task is spoken of as an up-hill job. We talk of climbers and say of a man whose pretensions have suffered a rude shock that he had to "climb down." It is all the same symbolism and not very cryptic at that.

As for the names Jack and Jill, there is nothing definite to be gleaned from the many instances in literature where they are found together. Wither (4),

Ben Jonson (5), Shakespeare (6), Kendal (7), Skelton (8), and the old ballad makers (9) mention Jack and Jill, but there is no evidence that they refer to the rhyme. It appears that these are generic names standing for man and woman or lad and lass.

Jill or Gyll, is short for Gillian, which is probably the same as Juliana. It was in quite common use up to the end of the sixteenth century, is only rarely met with in the next fifty years, and has quite died out since that time. Jack has survived in everyday speech as the familiar form of John.

Now if there is any real significance in the phrase "broke his crown," it calls for a review of the long list of English kings. Sure enough, there is a King John—and only one. He was hated by his people, he set out on a foolish and difficult enterprise, he failed, he lost his crown, and there was general rejoicing at his fall. Unfortunately for this type of inquiry, John reigned at the very beginning of the thirteenth century. At that early date written records are very few and those few chiefly are found in monkish Latin or the Norman French of the court. The English of the period was rude and barbaric, for not many could read or write; it was still the grey dawn of literature in England. No one with a conscience would choose such an age for historical research; there are too few sources of contemporary evidence.

With a heavy handicap like this, the interpretation of the rhyme of Jack and Jill may offer a good many difficulties. In any case the pail of water calls for an explanation, and in all probability the cream of the jest is in that very phrase. The pail of water is the object of Jack's up-hill struggle, a ludicrous goal at best; if Jack is King John the phrase ought to conceal, by means of pun or quibble, the real purpose for which he risked his crown.

The word *water* may give us a clue. There is only one possible double meaning and that is a pun on a name, which is some encouragement for the baffled antiquary. Nowadays when we say talk or walk we do not pronounce the letter "l" which is carefully retained in the spelling of the words. In the same way, at an early period of English, the "l" was silent before "t" as well as "k." Later on, the sound was restored in speech so that we now say Walter where formerly one said Water. The Scotch dialect, which is often a survival of middle English usage, still ignores the "l" before "t." The common English family name Waters and the Scotch name Watt are merely relics of the old pronunciation of Walter.

There was no prejudice in the past against a play upon words. Gentle folk and peasants alike took delight in punning and the identity of sound in water and Walter was often the occasion of a jest. For instance, in the vault of Norwich cathedral may be seen carved in stone the figure of a stag crouching in a stream. It is a punning rebus and the syllables represented are water, lie, and hart—the signature of Walter Lyhart.

Shakespeare was not ashamed to use the same double meaning in his play of Henry VI. The ambitious Suffolk has consulted an astrologer who told him that he should get his death by water. Later, when disgraced and outlawed, Suffolk is trying to escape from England in disguise. He is caught and tries to arrange for a ransom, when one of his captors remarks:

> "my name is Walter Whitmore
> How now! Why start'st thou? What, doth
> death affright?"

Suffolk replies:

> "Thy name affrights me in whose sound is death
> A cunning man did calculate my birth
> And told me that by water I should die." (10)

Suffolk is recognized and, sure enough, he meets his death at the hands of this same Walter.

Accordingly we must find a man named Walter concerned in the events which the rhyme celebrates. Really, this problem is growing more and more involved: it is like a detective story with new and highly suspicious characters introduced with every chapter. However, there is some comfort in the thought that a political riddle would hardly mention anyone obscure or lowly. To be recognized in a punning rhyme this Walter must have been well-known to all the common people of his age. Luckily, there are only a limited number of men named Walter eminent enough in English history to meet the requirement of our theory.

To be logical, any attempt at identification must connect this character with the pail. After all, Jack set out on his unfortunate quest to get the pail of Walter, whatever that may mean, and there's no dodging the issue. Unless a meaning can be found which will link up the figures of the rhyme to make a connected story, all this theorizing will prove to have been an idle gesture.

There is a Latin word *pallium* which means the sacred vestment of an archbishop. This word appears in early English as pael, paelle, and paile, with the later form pel shifting over to the modern pronunciation pall. (11) Layamon, who wrote in 1205, has the form pael. This pallium was the symbol of the office and dignity of an archbishop just as a mitre stood for any bishop in the realm. Heraldic devices served in the illiterate ages to identify the great and the powerful; men could read armorial bearings when they could not read written words. What was the coat-of-arms of the archbishops of Canterbury? Simply a shield of azure on which was charged a pallium like a broad white Y. In past centuries the archbishop of Canterbury held a position of extraordinary power in affairs of the state as well as of the church. Yet everyone knew that although elected to the office he was powerless and without authority until he had received from the pope the sacred investiture of the pallium. (12)

Clearly, we must find a certain Walter who was an archbishop and discover if we can why Jack and Jill wanted to get his pael. This archbishop, too, must prove to have lived in an age when a pallium was called a pael and not a pall. Finally, it must be shown that the whole affair of Jack, Jill, Walter's pael and the breaking of the crown was a story of absorbing interest to the common people who hid in rhyming riddles their dislike of prelate and king.

In the closing years of the twelfth century one figure looms as the greatest Englishman of his age. This man was Hubert Walter. King Richard of the Lionhart, who made him bishop of Salisbury, took him as his right-hand man on the third crusade to the Holy Land. In 1193, Richard left him in Palestine in command of the English army with orders to bring home the remnant of the crusaders. Once more in England, Hubert Walter found all the power of the realm in his hands. Richard was a prisoner in Austria, and Walter, now archbishop of Canterbury and Justiciar of England, faced the task of governing the country in the name of the king and of raising by taxation the enormous ransom needed for Richard's release. Meanwhile, Richard's younger brother, Prince John, had been conspiring to usurp the throne. In 1194 this treachery came to a head and Walter set to work loyally to defend the rights of Richard, his friend and his king.

As archbishop he excommunicated John, as Justiciar he declared his property forfeited to the crown, as lieutenant general he led an army against the black-hearted Prince and was winning castle after castle when King Richard at last came back to England. John cringed to the generous Richard for a pardon and was taken back into favor as his heir. Richard was soon away again to fight new wars in France, and for four years Hubert Walter was virtually king while John sulked in his castle. When Richard died in 1199 it was Archbishop Walter who, on Ascension day, crowned John as king of England. Although he feared and hated Walter, John was too weak to govern alone; the power of the archbishop was too real and too necessary, and the chancellor of the new reign was Hubert Walter.

When King John proposed to raise forces for another aimless war in France, the chancellor was steadfast in opposition and the project was abandoned. Walter had once more scored over the weakling John -- who resolved to get an archbishop, if he might, who would do his bidding. Hubert Walter died in 1205. "Now," said King John, "for the first time am I truly King of England!" (13)

As the new archbishop of Canterbury, the king chose John de Grey, bishop of Norwich, a wretched creature whom he had made royal treasurer. To the priors at Christ Church at Canterbury were sent orders to elect John de Grey; but in the meantime they had met in secret and elected their sub-prior, Reginald, who was already on his way to Rome to receive the pallium from the pope.

Now Pope Innocent III was no fool and he flatly refused to recognize John's candidate. Reginald, though, was a poor stick and would never do as the pope's representative in England. So Innocent told the Christ Church priors to elect Stephen Langton on whose shoulders the pope felt safe in laying the pallium of archbishop. John, in his turn, defied the pope, made John de Grey the chief of his council, and drove the priors of Christ Church out of the kingdom.

And so the issue was drawn between pope and king on the question—who was to get the pael of Walter. That quarrel was what split the kingdom and lost John his crown. (14)

The pope's first move was to lay all England under an interdict; all the churches were closed, there were no sacraments save in secret. When John retorted by seizing the property of churchmen who obeyed the pope, the people of England sided with the church against the tyranny of the king. The few bishops who followed "that beast of Norwich," John de Grey, and served King John, were ridiculed in punning jingles. They were greedy for gold; churchmen who cared more for marks than for Mark, priests who loved lucre rather than Luke. (15)

The interdict was bad enough, but the pope's next move was more serious still; he excommunicated John.

Jack and Jill

Still the king blustered. Finally, Pope Innocent declared that he would depose King John. The people were murmuring against him, his barons hated his falseness and cruelty, his power in his own realm had melted away. John had no choice but to submit. On the eve of Ascension day of the year 1213, King John swore to acknowledge Langton as archbishop of Canterbury and gave up his crown to the hands of the legate of the pope.

This Langton, by the way, (the man who got the pael of Walter, after all) had the same weakness for bad puns as the other Englishmen of his time. The proof is to be found in Canterbury cathedral where his rebus may be seen today carved in the stonework of his tomb. Here and there in the tracery stands the figure of a slender barrel or long tun, the signature of Langton.

King John, of course, is Jack. But who is Jill? One would naturally expect to find a woman in the case; but, while there were many women in King John's life, there was not one of them willing to share his fall. More than that, if he started out with one when he went up the hill, it was quite another by the time he fell and broke his crown. On second thought it will be clear that it was for no woman's sake that John attempted to brazen the pope and control the see of Canterbury.

King John wanted the pael of Walter for John de Grey. It was with him that the king set out on this disastrous venture and when John's crown broke, the bishop of Norwich came tumbling after. Nothing was left him; his enemies were in the saddle; he was disgraced and excommunicated. Poor John de Grey, sick at heart, set out on a weary pilgrimage to Rome to beg absolution at the feet of the pope, and England never saw him again.

There is nothing in the record of history to show that he was ever known as Jill. Yet there are many instances where a churchman has been named in derision and contempt as a woman. The long gown, the smooth face, the vow of chastity, the cloistered life— all these gave occasion to the ribald for giving a woman's character and a woman's name to a man of the church.

Furthermore, the word Jill implied very commonly a person of no character, mercenary and faithless. (16) Our word jilt is only a contemptuous diminutive of the word jill. Such qualities might fairly be ascribed to John de Grey. He had prostituted his office for gain, betrayed his church and ranked as an apostate from his faith. The proverbial example of such conduct was Julian the Apostate; if the bishop of Norwich was compared with Julian, there would be an opening for the derisive epithet of Jill. In any case, the rhyme tells the story of two Johns; both could not be called Jack without confusion of sense. It would be an easy and natural transition to Jack and Jill.

It is a pity that there have not been preserved some of the popular rhymes of the period. We only know rather vaguely that King John's defeat was predicted in verse by the common people of England. Shakespeare in his play of King John shows Fauconbridge reporting to the king:

> But as I travell'd hither through the land,
> I find the people strangely fantasied;
> Possess'd with rumours, full of idle dreams,
> Not knowing what they fear, but full of fear:
> And here's a prophet that I brought with me
> From forth the streets of Pomfret, whom I found
> With many hundreds treading on his heels;
> To whom he sung in rude harsh-sounding rhymes,
> That ere the next Ascension-day at noon,
> Your highness should deliver up your crown. (17)

It is rather suggestive how closely Ascension day was associated with King John in the minds of the people; on Ascension day he was crowned; on Ascension day he was brought low. It may be straining a point, perhaps, to think that this association influenced the choice of the figure of speech "went up the hill."

If there was at first this political meaning in the rhyme of Jack and Jill, why should we not find some passing reference, at least, in the course of the ensuing seven hundred years? One reason may be that for three centuries after John's fall there is no body of literature that gives any reflection of the thoughts of the ordinary average man or woman. By that time the double meaning was in part obsolete and the original sense forgotten. Yet in the first part of the sixteenth century there appeared a poem, The Image of Ipocrasie, in which are found lines that might imply a memory of the story of our rhyme:

> It is therefore great skill
> that every Iacke and gyll
> performe the pope's will. (18)

It may be pure coincidence, but there it is.

Any number of objections may be urged against this historical interpretation of the rhyme of Jack and Jill. For instance, it will be argued that the survival of an oral tradition from so distant a period of time would be very unlikely. True enough. Yet there is no lack of tales and ballads of Robin Hood and that popular hero flourished in an age even earlier than the time of King John.

The worst blow is the fact that an interpretation of Jack and Jill has already been given to the world. In 1866 the Rev. Sabine Baring-Gould wrote his Curious Myths of the Middle Ages in which he claimed that the rhyme of Jack and Jill is a fragment of the Old Norse Edda. It is only fair to give him a hearing. This is his thesis:

"Mani, the moon, stole two children from their parents, and carried them up to heaven. Their names were Hjuki and Bil. They had been drawing water from the well Byrgir, in the bucket Soegr, suspended from the pole Simul, which they bore upon their shoulders. These children, pole and bucket, were placed in heaven 'where they could be seen from earth.' This refers undoubtedly to the spots in the moon, and so the Swedish peasantry explain these spots to this day as representing a boy and a girl bearing a pail of water between them. Are we not reminded at once of our nursery rhyme—

> 'Jack and Jill went up a hill
> To fetch a pail of water:
> Jack fell down and broke his crown
> And Jill came tumbling after'?

"This verse, which to us seems at first sight nonsense, I have no hesitation in saying has a high antiquity, and refers to the Eddaic Hjuki and Bil. The names indicate as much. Hjuki, in Norse, would be pronounced Juki, which would readily become Jack; and Bil for the sake of euphony, and in order to give a female name to one of the children, would become Jill. The fall of Jack and the subsequent fall of Jill simply represent the vanishing of one moon spot after another as the moon wanes." (19)

The danger in this kind of investigation—Baring-Gould's and mine—is that it is easy in any form of research to find what you are looking for. Interest in one's theory grows naturally into enthusiasm, which easily becomes indifferent to facts which point in another direction. There is no object in debating the value of the two interpretations. It may be simply a matter of whether one prefers mythology or history. There is a serious lack of confirmatory evidence in either case for the origin of Jack and Jill. I would bring in the old Scotch verdict—NOT PROVEN.

REFERENCES

GOOSEY GANDER

1) Ben Jonson: Execr. of Vulcan. Vol. VI, p. 410.
2) Wm. Shakespeare: Henry VI. Part I, Act I, Sc. III.
3) John Foxe: Acts and Monuments. (Ed. A. Clarke) Book VIII, p. 639.
4) J. A. Muller: Stephen Gardiner and the Tudor Reaction. p. 114, 125, 243, 257, 269.
5) Furnivall: Ballads from Manuscripts. p. 473, note.
6) S. Hubert Burke: Historical Portraits of the Tudor Dynasty. Vol. II, p. 9.
7) J. Gairdner: Lollardy and the Reformation. Vol. III, p. 31.
8) J. A. Froude: History of England. Vol. VI, p. 87, note.
9) Strype: Memorials of Cranmer. p. 456.

THE MAN IN THE MOON

S. R. Gardiner: History of the Great Civil War.
――――――― History of the Commonwealth and Protectorate.

1) New English Dictionary.
2) T. B. Macaulay: History of England. Vol. I, p. 392; vol. II, p. 97.
   H. E. Rollins: Cavalier and Puritan. p. 160, note.
3) Dictionary of National Biography: Godwin.
4) Robert Burton: Anatomy of Melancholy. Vol. I, p. 11.
   J. P. Williams: History of English Journalism. p. 94, 119.
   Michael Drayton: Endymion (concluding lines).
5) Bulstrode Whitelock: Memorials of the English Affairs. p. 308.
6) Samuel Butler: Hudibras (Bohn edition). p. 2, note 3.
7) New English Dictionary.
8) Walter Scott: Pontefract Castle. Chap. IV and XI.
9) Bulstrode Whitelock: Memorials of the English Affairs. p. 311.
10) Samuel Butler: Hudibras. Part II, Canto II, l. 858.
11) Samuel Butler: Hudibras. Part II, Canto III, l. 767.

References

THE LION AND THE UNICORN

S. R. Gardiner: History of the Commonwealth and Protectorate. (Referred to below as S. R. G.)

1) Fabyan's Chronicle. p. 672.
2) George Wither: Abuses Stript and Whipt. Book 2. Satire 1. Vanitie. Line 173 seq.
3) Encyclopedia Britannica: Unicorn.
4) Ed. Spenser: Fairie Queene. Book II, Canto V, Verse X.
5) S.R.G. Vol. II, p. 2.
6) Terry: History of England. p. 723.
7) S.R.G. Vol. II, p. 310.
8) S.R.G. Vol. III, p. 187.
9) Gilbert Burnet: The History of My Own Time. p. 35.
10) Bulstrode Whitelock: Memorials of the English Affairs. p. 483.
11) S.R.G. Vol. II, p. 67.
    Nicoll's Diary. p. 80.
12) Another Victory, quoted by S.R.G. Vol. I, p. 461.
13) S.R.G. Vol. I, p. 465, seq.
14) Gilbert Burnet: The History of My Own Time. p. 386.

HUMPTY DUMPTY

1) Mother Goose's Melodies: Ed. Wm. A. Wheeler.
2) Line Eckenstein: Comparative Studies in Nursery Rhymes. p. 104 seq.
3) Richard Bentley: Dissertation on Phalaris. p. xl.
4) Bentley. p. xxi.
5) Bentley. p. xx.
6) Frey: Sobriquets and Nicknames. p. 158.
7) New English Dictionary: Humpty-dumpty.
8) Robert Fabyan: The New Chronicles of England and France. p. 672.
9) Variorum Shakespeare: Ed. Furness. King Richard the Third. p. 98 note (quoted from Heywood Edward IV p. 177: Ed. Pearson).
10) New English Dictionary: set.
11) E. Cobham Brewer: The Readers' Handbook. p. 1186.
12) James Halliwell-Phillips: Dictionary of Archaic and Provincial words. (dumpty) and (humpty).
13) Thomas More: History of King Richard the Third. p. 5.
14) More. p. 52 seq.
15) New English Dictionary: cast.
16) Sharon Turner: History of England during the Middle Ages. Vol. IV, p. 101 and note.
17) Wm. Shakespeare: King Richard the Third. Act V, scene 3, line 305.
18) Turner. Vol. IV, p. 36, 44 and note.

References

19) Hall's Chronicle. p. 418.
20) Grafton's Chronicle. Vol. II, p. 154.
21) Wm. Shakespeare: King Richard the Third. Act V, Scene 4, line 13.
22) Michael Drayton: Works. Vol. II Poly-olbion: Song of the twenty-second, p. 1100.

MISTRESS MARY

1) Thos. Wright: Political Poems and Songs. Vol. II, p. 269.
2) J. A. Froude: The Divorce of Catherine of Aragon. p. 239.
3) New English Dictionary.
4) J. A. Froude: History of England. Vol. V, p. 308, note.
5) Froude: The Divorce of Catherine of Aragon. p. 271.
6) J. M. Stone: History of Mary I. p. 157.
7) S. Hubert Burke: Historical Portraits of the Tudor Dynasty. Vol. II, p. 512.
8) Sharon Turner: History of the Reigns of Edward VI, Mary and Elizabeth. Vol. I, p. 322.
9) J. A. Froude: History of England. Vol. V, p. 309.
10) Nugae Antiquae. Vol. II, p. 78.
11) J. A. Muller: Stephen Gardiner and the Tudor Reaction. p. 126.
12) Nugae Antiquae. Vol. VI, p. 78, note.
13) J. A. Muller: Stephen Gardiner.... p. 86.
14) Percy's Reliques. Vols. II, XVIII.
15) John Foxe: Acts and Monuments (ed. A. Clarke). Book VI, p. 359.
16) Furnivall: Ballads from Manuscripts. Vol. I.
17) Robert Burton: Anatomy of Melancholy. Vol. III, p. 424.
18) Nugae Antiquae. Vol. II, p. 3.
19) J. A. Froude: History of England. Vol. V, p. 424 seq.
20) Froude (note 19, above).

21) Froude: History of England. Vol. VI, p. 43 seq.
22) Machyn's Diary. 1553.
23) Froude: History of England. Vol. VI, p. 102.

HARK HARK

1) G. M. Trevelyan: England under the Stuarts. p. 28.
2) J. J. Jusserand: English Wayfaring Life. p. 115.
3) Thomas Wright: Political Poems and Songs. Vol. II, p. 30.
4) Hall's Chronicle. p. 593.
5) J. A. Froude: History of England. Vol. II, p. 438.
6) Sharon Turner: History of the Reign of Henry VIII. Vol. II, p. 359, note.

WILLIAM AND MARY

1) J. O. Halliwell-Phillips: The Nursery Rhymes of England. Vol. IV, p. 10.
2) Mother Goose's Melodies: Ed. W. A. Wheeler. p. 160 and note.
3) John Booth: Epigrams Ancient and Modern. p. 86.
4) Mother Goose's Melodies: Ed. W. A. Wheeler. p. 152 and note.
5) Jacobite Minstrelsy. Glasgow. Richard Griffen & Co. 1829. p. 28.
6) Earl Stanhope: History of England comprising the reign of Queen Anne. Vol. I, p. 43.
7) Gilbert Burnet: The History of My Own Time. p. 833 and note.
8) Supplement to Burnet's History of My Own Time. p. 142.
9) Burnet: History of My Own Time. p. 154.
10) Andrew Marvell: Poetical Works. p. 164.
11) Burnet. p. 476.
12) Burnet. p. 902, note.
13) Supplement to Burnet. p. 276.
14) Daniel DeFoe: Review (1711). Vii, p. 587.
15) Clarendon Correspondence. Vol. II, p. 208.
16) John Bramston: Autobiography. p. 341.
17) Burnet. p. 508, note.
18) Stanhope. Vol. I, p. 10.
19) Walter Wilson: Memoirs of the Life and Times of Daniel DeFoe. Vol. II, p. 233.
20) Jacobite Minstrelsy. p. 7.

JACK AND JILL

1) John Evelyn: Diary. Vol. IV, p. 205.
2) Percy's Reliques. Vol. II, p. 291.
3) Percy's Reliques. Vol. I, p. 209.
4) George Wither: Christmas Carroll.
5) Ben Jonson: Gipsies metamorphosed.
6) Shakespeare: Love's Labour's Lost. Act V, Scene 2, line 805.
    Midsummer Night's Dream. Act III, Scene 2, 1. 461.
7) Timothe Kendal: Flowers of Epigrammes (Spencer Society). p. 196.
8) John Skelton: Colyn Cloute. line 260.
9) Thos. Wright: Political Poems and Songs. Vol. II, p. 250.
    Percy's Reliques. Vol. II, p. 155.
10) Shakespeare: King Henry VI. Part II, Act IV, Sc. 1.
11) New English Dictionary: pall.
12) Fabyan's Chronicle. I, ccxxi.
13) Matthew Paris: Historia Anglorum (Rolls Series) II, 104.
14) Paris. II, 493.
15) S. R. Gardiner: A Student's History of England. p. 178.
16) Nicholas Udall: Ralph Roister Doister. Act III, Scene 4, line 105.
17) Timothe Kendall: Flowers of Epigrammes (Spencer Society). p. 196.
    Shakespeare: King John. Act. IV, Sc. 2.
18) John Skelton: Works (ed. Dyce). The Image of Ipocrasie. Part II.
19) Baring-Gould: Curious Myths of the Middle Ages.